MW00333388

GHOSTS OF MICHIGAN'S UPPER PENINSULA

JENNIFER BILLOCK

Haunted
America

Published by Haunted America
A Division of The History Press
Charleston, SC
www.historypress.com

First published 2018

ISBN 9781540236067

Library of Congress Control Number: 2018943599

Notice: The information in this book is true and complete to the best of our knowledge. It is offered without guarantee on the part of the author or The History Press. The author and The History Press disclaim all liability in connection with the use of this book.

For my dearly departed friends and family,
who I hope are relentlessly haunting me.

CONTENTS

CONTENTS

ACKNOWLEDGEMENTS

First, a big thanks to anyone who's ever had to sit through a conversation with me that's been punctuated with pauses for me to say, "That's a great story/book idea..." and then pull out my phone to write it down in my notes. And yes, that's pretty much every single person I know. Your patience and support of my creative impulses are so appreciated.

This book came to life with a lot of help. In no particular order, I'd like to thank Frederick Stonehouse, Anthony Douglas, Calvin Staricha, Jesse Land, Coriane Penegor and the Ontonagon County Historical Society, the ever-fabulous team at Michigan Tech's archives, Hilary Billman and the Marquette Maritime Museum, Rick from the Crisp Point Light Historical Society, Chris Szabo, Derek Hall at Northern Michigan University, Todd Clements from the Haunts of Mackinac Tour Company, Craig Nuottila, Heather Tamlyn, Wayne Peacock, Brad Blair, Paul Sabourin, Lynn at the Calumet Theatre, the amazing Patty Pattison, Jeremiah Mason, a whole slew of folks on Facebook (Kathleen Fairbanks, Thomas Read, Katie Hatcher, Linda St. Germain, John David Arnold, Susan Wickstrom, Betsie Reed, Pam Gramling, Judy O'Betts, Darla Manninen, Holly Stromer, Tasha Paavola, Cheryl Rotole, Mary Beyers, Danielle Adams, Brenda Niemela, Makayala Isaacson, Priscilla Ross-Fox, Joe Gervais, Mary Ciurro, Jean Butler, Joan Fischer, Tony Roseman, Lynn Lanyon, Edwin Wakeham, Amy Jeffery, Ellen Vangemert, Robert Grizz and more) and, as always, my constantly supportive family and friends.

THE ETHEREAL UPPER PENINSULA

A sk someone who frequents Michigan's Upper Peninsula, and you'll hear it called a multitude of things: the Northwoods, God's Country, the Yoop, Up North and more. It's a favorite place for people looking for a bit of solitude, a break from the everyday. If you want to get away into nature, just head north.

The travelers heading up are right—you'll be hard-pressed to find anybody who interrupts your time at the lake or your camp. And that's because the small UP, which holds one-third of the land in Michigan, also only holds 3 percent of the population. Census numbers have been on a steady decline since the mining boom, when Calumet, now a town of only 706 people, almost became the state capital.

Hundreds of thousands of immigrants flocked to the Upper Peninsula in its heyday. They took up jobs in the copper or iron mines, in the fishing outfits or at the lumberyards and sawmills. Summer cottages sprang up for the workers to vacation at, and a rich history of lake life began. But then the industries started to fade, and the people made a mass exodus.

But they left behind a rich heritage. From the abandoned mining towns and the remnants of Finnish culture in the west to the ore pocket docks and lifesaving stations in the east and along the coast, the Upper Peninsula still holds the heart of the people who forged the land before us.

And, some say, the souls as well. During the boom years, the UP saw an enormous amount of death. Mines collapsed, murders shocked the small towns and an entire legion of mariners drowned at sea. All the casualties were reborn in a new form: ghosts, spirits and the occasional monster.

INTRODUCTION

Among these pages, you'll find some of the most well-known ghost stories to haunt the Upper Peninsula, as well as some of the more hidden mysteries. Historical research and personal accounts demystify many of these paranormal tales—whether that means we finally learn who the real ghost is at Northern Michigan University's fine arts building or we learn that one of the peninsula's most famous hauntings is not so supernatural at all. Here you'll read of ghosts and graveyards, shipwrecks and specters, UFOs and undead souls. You'll learn that even though much of the Upper Peninsula appears deserted, the history and haunts of the past will never truly be able to leave.

PART I

WESTERN UPPER PENINSULA HAUNTS

THE ITALIAN HALL AND THE CALUMET THEATRE

The cold winter moon still rises to find
A trace of the old Calumet Copper Mine
And the place where the children were waiting inside
For legend to freeze them in time.

The Keweenaw wind blows lonesome and cold
It cuts to the marrow and chills to the soul
With the memory of children like yours and like mine
Too young to be frozen in time.
—"Frozen in Time," Larry Penn

Christmas Eve 1913 in Calumet was meant to be a time of laughter, fun and presents for union miners and their families. There'd been a labor strike on for five months at that point, and it was high time for a little holiday cheer. The women's union group knew it, so it organized a massive holiday party for that night, held upstairs at the Italian Hall, a large red brick building at the corner of Elm and Seventh Streets.

More than six hundred people packed into the building for the festivities. The majority were children, either with their parents, their siblings or their friends. At the start, it was a fabulous time. The children sang Christmas carols, dancing and laughing with their friends. Santa had just come in, and kids were pushing to the stage to receive their gifts from under the big Christmas tree. Sadly, those presents would never make their way home.

Shortly after Santa arrived, a large bearded man pushed open the door to the hall and screamed, "Fire!" The spark of fear moved fast, and suddenly everyone was rushing to the one exit: a narrow staircase heading down to the front door of the building. The fire escape mostly went unnoticed in the mayhem. Terror propelled the revelers forward, shoving and pushing to the door, knocking over and trampling smaller bodies and the adults who stooped to pick them up. Some were crushed to death against the door of a cloakroom next to the staircase.

But those who made it to the stairs first had the worst fate. In the rush to escape, both children and adults were shoved from the steps and thrown down the stairs, landing against closed doors at the bottom. It continued in that fashion—whoever hit the landing was tossed into the stairway—and bodies piled atop one another. Newspapers at the time reported that the stairwell was filled to the ceiling with suffocating and crushed people. The doors at the bottom never opened to let anyone out.

The mayhem only lasted a few moments before those present realized that there was no fire, but it was long enough for massive casualties. All told, seventy-three people lost their lives that night by crushing or suffocation—fifty-nine children and fourteen adults. The youngest victim was only two years old.

The man who raised the fire alarm was never found. True to the union disputes at the time, rumors swirled that he was wearing an anti-union button. Many thought that he was sent by the mine bosses to break up the party as retaliation for the miners not working. Today, it is still one of the Upper Peninsula's biggest unsolved crimes.

Not much of the Italian Hall remains today, save for the arched doorway that still stands at the same spot, a folding chair from the event space and a single step from the stairs where so many met their fate. The step and chair are part of an exhibit at the Calumet Visitor Center; to place your hand on the step is to make a physical connection with the historic tragedy. You can almost feel the wrenching emotion felt by so many on the night of that party pulsing through your hand as you touch it.

A similar intensity fills the air at the actual site of the hall, where the arched doorway remains as part of a memorial park. Although the building itself is no longer there, the community honors the spirits of the dead

Outside the Italian Hall, before the 1913 disaster. *Michigan Technological University Archives and Copper Country Historical Collections.*

inside with seventy-three luminaries, lit every Christmas Eve on a path on the way to the arch.

After the catastrophe, bodies of the dead were moved a block away to the Red Jacket Town Hall and Opera House, now the Calumet Theatre, which worked as a temporary morgue. It took hours to identify all the

Left: The fatal entryway where most died in the Italian Hall disaster. *Michigan Technological University Archives and Copper Country Historical Collections.*

Below: A step from the staircase where so many unfortunate souls met their fate in the Italian Hall.

bodies, compounded by false recognitions from distraught parents amid all the confusion and chaos. Mothers in the street were screaming out for their lost children in the hopes they had survived, while inside, parents were taking away bodies of what they thought were their own children, only to return with the body later after finding theirs alive and well.

More than twenty thousand people came to Calumet for the victims' mass burial on December 28, 1913. Caskets had been shipped in from surrounding towns, and simple pine boxes were also constructed for burials. At the nearby Lakeview Cemetery, striking miners dug trench graves for all the bodies. A handful of local churches hosted funerals. Afterward, everyone filed outside, marching down Pine Street in a massive procession of mourners, with union members carrying caskets of children and horse-drawn hearses holding adult coffins. Thousands walked with the procession to the cemetery, where a multilingual graveside service continued past sunset and into the evening.

Victims' caskets waiting inside a church for the mass funeral procession. *Michigan Technological University Archives and Copper Country Historical Collections.*

The Calumet Theatre was a makeshift morgue for the bodies from the Italian Hall disaster. *Calumet Theatre.*

Some locals say, though, that even after the bodies were identified and buried, some of the victims never left that temporary morgue in the theater. Someone walking by or going to an event inside needs only to quietly listen to hear the reported laughter of children as they play, as well as the screams of those who realize what's happened to them.

Unlike the Italian Hall, the Calumet Theatre is still standing, and it is haunted by its own set of original ghosts in addition to the spectral children of the Italian Hall disaster. The theater opened in the heyday of Calumet's history; at the time, about four thousand people lived in the village itself, and more than thirty thousand were a quick walk away. Great fanfare accompanied the first performance on March 20, 1900: a touring Broadway show, Reginald DeKoven's *The Highwaymen*. For the next thirty or so years, American theater greats filled the stage, performers like Sarah Bernhardt, John Philip Sousa, Lillian Russell and William S. Hart.

But in the late 1920s, the Depression began to take hold. Copper mining in the area was on the decline, as was the population as residents left to find work elsewhere. Stage shows stopped, and the theater became the local movie theater. It ran that way until 1972, when Michigan State University acquired the building. The auditorium and building were renovated, restored and brought up to code. Now, the theater is run by the Calumet Theatre Company, a nonprofit cultural organization that brings in shows and works on continuing restoration. Some big names (like Bob Milne, Lee Greenwood and the Glenn Miller Orchestra) have returned to the theater, which now hosts up to sixty-five events annually that draw about eighteen thousand people.

At least one performer from the early days of the theater's history, though, apparently decided to stay on the company roster. Renowned Shakespearean actress Madame Helena Modjeska had a good enough time at her three performances there in the early 1900s that she never left. Her haunting of the theater first emerged in 1958. The site was hosting a stage production of *The Taming of the Shrew* on July 22 that year. One of the stars, actress Addyse Lane, was partway through her soliloquy as Kate in Act V,

The ghost of Madame Helena Modjeska helps actresses struggling with their lines in this auditorium. *Calumet Theatre.*

Scene 2, when her mind went blank. She began to adlib in an attempt to find her missing line. Modjeska must have been distraught at the idea of a Shakespeare play gone awry, for Lane reported after the performance that a bright light appeared on the balcony and floated down to her at the stage. Modjeska herself reached out of the glow and whispered Lane's line to her. Lane was able to finish the show without any more mistakes thanks to the helpful apparition.

Since that performance, reports of Modjeska's presence appear every year. Generally, it's just a quick sighting, but some have suggested poltergeist activity related to the actress. Her portrait hangs on the wall in the theater, and she gets pretty mad if the picture comes down; its removal is inevitably followed by flickering lights and loud crashes.

Frequent patrons of the theater, though, are quick to point out that Modjeska isn't the only spirit walking the building's halls. From the reports, it sounds like there's actually a whole afterlife party happening. The staff, including the executive director and the technical crew, have all reported hearing unexplained music playing from different parts of the theater, mysteriously locked and rattling door handles, cold breezes and ghostly figures on the stage and balconies. Visitors on tours claim to have seen ectoplasm floating in the balcony and on the stage and felt ghostly taps on the shoulder. And one of the resident ghosts seems to be a bit of a trickster—once, during a bingo game going on in the theater, the players heard a voice from across the room shouting, "Bingo!"

Not all the spirits in the theater are quite so jovial, though. Two unconfirmed 1903 murders took place here—one of an unnamed man and one of a young girl named Elanda Rowe—although no records exist to prove them, save for the screams locals and visitors alike hear coming from different parts of the theater.

MINING TOWNS AND MINESHAFTS

In 1843, a mineral boom struck Michigan's Upper Peninsula. It was the country's first rush to gather raw copper, iron and silver and the first time miners converged on one specific area of the United States (the California Gold Rush started five years later, in 1848). Thousands of prospective miners hoping to make a life in the wild Northwoods flocked to the region from around the world. More than 250 mines popped up during the height of the boom, and along with that, a mass of mine towns was hastily built to house the workers. Old Victoria was one such place.

The Victoria Mine first opened in 1849 as the Cushin Mine. Cushin operated for nine years before reorganizing into the Victoria Mining Company. This iteration of the mine ran on and off until 1899, when it was reorganized yet again to be the Victoria Copper Mining Company. Work in the mine then took off in earnest. Twenty cabins were built that year for miners and their families. At peak operation in 1917, more than fifty company buildings and houses composed the mine, with a population estimated at about 750. The mine itself was only a half mile deep, but it was spread out lengthwise underground, encompassing the entire area underneath the company town.

Helia Arvola standing in front of the house she grew up in at the Victoria Mine. *Old Victoria Association.*

Deaths in mining towns were common, and Victoria was no exception. The mine ran until 1921, and during that time, twenty-five men died underground. But according to Patty Pattison, the site manager at the Old Victoria restoration site, more children died in the town than those lost in the mine. Old age, disease and childbirth complications were leading causes of death for both women and children living in Victoria.

Today, the remains of Victoria are substantially sparser than the once booming mine town. Four houses have been restored, and the Old Victoria Society maintains the site. Ruins still lie at rest in the woods, subject only to nature and the watchful eyes of guests touring the property. But in the houses, particularly one that at one point belonged to the Arvola family, the life of a miner's wife continues on.

On March 25, 1911, Johanna Arvola was on her deathbed. She was struggling through a dangerous pregnancy and eventual miscarriage. The Victoria Company doctor had been by her side for the past two days, and each of her seven children (ranging in age from two to fifteen) had taken their turn visiting their dying mother before she passed at 9:00 p.m. She was only thirty-nine when she died.

It's important to note that Johanna's death certificate doesn't list "miscarriage" as a cause of death; instead, it says "abortion." Pattison says this is due to the era. In 1911, when Johanna died, doctors used the term *abortion* frequently when a woman lost a baby before twenty weeks. Johanna's pregnancy was high risk—she was older and had already been pregnant ten times (with only seven living children). There is no evidence that she deliberately tried to abort her child.

Johanna is buried at Woodlawn Cemetery in nearby Rockland, along with her husband and several of their children. After her passing, the family stayed in Victoria, carrying on their mother's tradition of hospitality; she often took in boarders who stayed upstairs and shared meals at the family dinner table. Two of the Arvola boys went to work at the mine with their father, while the girls remained at home to care for the younger siblings. Eventually, the family moved away, although the eldest Arvola daughter, Helia, married a miner and continued to live at Victoria until its closure in 1921.

But Johanna's legacy doesn't end there. In 1973, Helia helped found the Society for the Restoration of Old Victoria. Her childhood home was still standing, and she spent hours during the restoration process regaling workers with intimate details about the house and life as a copper miner's daughter. When the site restoration was completed in 1976, she was there to cut the ribbon alongside two of her siblings.

The front bedroom, where Johanna Arvola died. *Old Victoria Association.*

Not long after, strange things began to happen in the Arvola house. Reports emerged of doors spontaneously slamming shut, moving shadows and stuck windows randomly opening. But the majority of stories surround a seemingly innocent piece of furniture: a rocking chair.

No one knows for sure exactly where the rocking chair came from. It was donated to the society as a piece of historical furniture that belonged to the Arvola family. Some think that Helia donated it, but a guest to the site once told Pattison that a man golfing in Florida said it was the rocker he was rocked in as a baby at Victoria—it's likely this man was one of the Arvola sons. The one thing known for sure about the rocking chair, though, is that it has a tendency to rock on its own. Both visitors and tour guides have seen the chair rock itself. According to legend, Johanna's ghost is sitting in the chair, rocking her miscarried baby to sleep.

The rocking chair and its ghostly occupant sometimes scare people so much that they refuse to go back into the house. Pattison told of a group of teens in the 1990s that volunteered with the society and usually stayed the night in the cabins. They were hanging out in the Arvola house at dusk when one of the girls decided to share the story of Johanna's ghost and the rocking chair. Pattison went to check on the group later that evening and found them all locked in a car, refusing to sleep in the house. Some of the girls were in tears from fear. Apparently, as the girl was telling Johanna's story, the group began to hear a baby cry. An apparition of a woman holding a child floated

The Arvola family in 1903. *From left to right*: William (seven), Johanna (thirty-three), Matt Jr. (five), Helia (four), Matt (forty-five) and Fannie (one). *Old Victoria Association.*

up in front of the group. The teens ran out and, to this day, refuse to sleep in that house.

Old Victoria is haunted by another ghost as well. Late at night—perhaps at the same time Johanna's rocking chair mysteriously begins to move—a lone miner walks down the street toward his home. He's seen better days; it's late, and he's ragged and tired from a long day at work. His lantern

The Arvola cabin (*left*) and the Usimaki cabin (*right*) in 1914. *Old Victoria Association.*

swings, lighting up the path around him and illuminating his most striking feature: half his face is missing. This ghostly miner is long dead, killed in an explosion at the mine that mars his face to this day.

The miner's identity remains a mystery. For a long time, staff and visitors thought that it was a man whose paycheck is on display at Old Victoria, but research showed that this particular man didn't perish in the mine. Luckily, that research also unearthed three miners who died in explosions at the mine, narrowing down the pool of potential ghostly candidates.

Thirty-three-year-old Onni is the first. He was a Finnish miner who died on April 3, 1907, after accidentally hitting a stick of dynamite with a pickaxe while underground. He survived a bit after the explosion, living to see the eighth floor of the mine—eight hundred feet below the surface and far out of reach of any available doctors. At the time of his death, he had a wife and four children. The entire family resided in one of the houses that still stands at Victoria. His teenage sister shared the family home at the time; it was she who signed Onni's death certificate. After his death, Onni's sister moved to another house and worked as a servant. The rest of the family remained in the original home until his wife remarried.

The ghostly walker could also be the spirit of twenty-eight-year-old Karl, another Finnish immigrant. He was working nights at the mine as a blaster when he died on April 8, 1912. The team in the mine had just charged thirty holes five levels down. Karl was a victim of circumstance—he was unable to get out of the way in time before the first hole exploded. The blast blew him seventy-five feet away, cracking his skull. He was killed instantly. Back at home, his wife and child waited fruitlessly in one of the houses for Karl's return. When they learned of his death, the mining company awarded his widow $1,200. Perhaps the most bitter part of Karl's tale is that the family had arrived from Finland only six months earlier. They came for a better life and instead found a tragic death.

Louis, the third potential ghost, was forty, Cornish and well accustomed to working in the mines. His seventeen-year-old son worked with him and witnessed the horrific accident that killed his father. At 4:00 a.m. on October 9, 1913, Louis drilled into a missed hole full of powder on the nineteenth level, causing an explosion that tore into his face. He lived an agonizing fifteen minutes following the blast. Unfortunately, death would continue to visit his surviving wife and four children. Seven months after Louis's death, his widow became ill and died. The kids stayed in the house at Victoria, but their grandmother arrived to care for them. She, too, died within a year of arriving at the house. After this last death, the children decided to leave the town for good.

The rest of the Victoria townsite has its spirits as well. Throughout the property, visitors claim to have seen moving shadows, heard whispers when no one was there and even seen full-body apparitions. One woman and her friend reported seeing two ghosts sitting on a woodpile. They took a photo, but the spirits did not appear—yet two ghostly shadows can be seen at the woodpile in the image. Pattison herself has experienced similar things at the site—most notably a ghostly orb led her to find initials she believes her great-uncle carved into one of the homes where her relatives once lived.

The Victoria Mine had its share of disasters in the early days, but none compares to the tragedy that happened in Mansfield, a mine cave-in that stands out in history as one of the area's worst calamities. The town of Mansfield sprang to life in 1889 when an explorer named W.S. Calhoun was contracted by the Caledonia Mining Company to hunt for iron ore around the banks of the Michigamme River. Find it he did, and Calhoun immediately leased the land from Caledonia to open the Mansfield Mine. About four hundred people packed up and headed to Mansfield, where, in addition to the mine, construction was underway on a school, a church and

Log House No. 10 at the Victoria Mine settlement before the restoration. *Old Victoria Association.*

several saloons, stores and boardinghouses. A rail line connected Mansfield to nearby Crystal Falls within a year, and by 1891, an official post office had opened in the town.

In 1893, the Mansfield Mine had 125 workers and a main shaft with six levels angled to the iron underneath the Michigamme. In all respects, Mansfield was a booming town, but one fateful night would alter the course of history there forever.

On September 28, a night crew of between forty-eight and sixty men left their homes for a shift at the mine. The group was used to hearing the rushing waters of the Michigamme overhead, as one of the shaft roofs was so close to the riverbed that, according to the Hudson Institute of Mineralogy, the men regularly heard logs scraping against the bottom of the river as they floated down to the sawmill. For a few days prior, the ceiling on the fifth level of the mine had been causing some trouble—as precaution, it had been secured with new timber as support for the weight above. None of the miners worried that it would cause an issue.

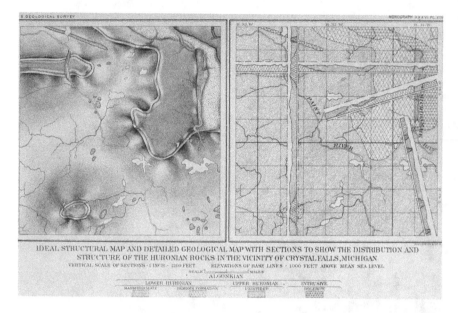

IDEAL STRUCTURAL MAP AND DETAILED GEOLOGICAL MAP WITH SECTIONS TO SHOW THE DISTRIBUTION AND STRUCTURE OF THE HURONIAN ROCKS IN THE VICINITY OF CRYSTAL FALLS, MICHIGAN
VERTICAL SCALE OF SECTIONS - 1 INCH - 1200 FEET   ELEVATIONS OF BASE LINES - 1000 FEET ABOVE MEAN SEA LEVEL

An early geological map showing distribution of iron deposits throughout the Crystal Falls and Mansfield areas.

When the crew descended into the mine, a few remarked that more water than usual appeared to be seeping in from the river. But again, there was no cause for alarm; mine safety standards required that the thickness of earth between the mine and the river was deep enough to make flooding impossible, and the upper levels, though all mined out, were secured with plenty of timber and ore pillars. And so the workers began their shift.

Shortly after work began, around 9:00 p.m., a crash and roar of water reverberated throughout the mine. The timbers holding up the fifth-floor roof had soaked through, and the ceiling collapsed. Without the supports beneath it, the four floors above each collapsed in succession. Water from the Michigamme poured into the mine. It rushed in so fast that the riverbed above the gaping hole ran dry.

The miners on the upper floors had no escape. If the falling roofs didn't crush them, the water deluged them and "drowned them like rats," one newspaper reported. Those on the lower levels were luckier. Andrew Sullivan, the night boss on the sixth level, heard the mayhem above and knew exactly what had happened—predictions of the roof caving in on the mine had been floating around for some time. He screamed at his charges to get to the ladder nearby. As they made their way, a rush of air ballooned into the mine, extinguishing every fire-powered light and lantern. The crew had to feel their way to and up the ladder in pitch darkness.

Escape for these men was harrowing. Water poured into the opening around the ladder, so they needed to hold their breath as they climbed to avoid drowning. They stopped at each level to step out of the waterfall and breathe before sucking in more air and starting another ascent. Four men were lost in the escape.

On the fourth floor, the skip tender, Tony Buletto, stood at the ready to help men escape up the shaft as the water poured in. He was with one of the night bosses, foreman Frank Rocco. Buletto urged Rocco to get in the skip with him so they could ride up to safety. But Rocco was responsible for his men and refused to escape until they'd been warned. He headed into the mine to tell them, but like his entire crew, he never again saw the light of day. Buletto made it to safety to tell of Rocco's heroism; he was the only man who survived from the fourth level.

Outside, Mansfield locals surrounded the cave-in site. They'd heard the crash from home and ran over to see the commotion. The night air was rife with screams and cries from wives left without husbands, children left without fathers and families left without sons and brothers. Men from the day shift volunteered to help with a rescue, but it was impossible to access the mine with the river rushing in.

By morning, the river had resumed its course, and the only evidence left of the cave-in was a reddish hue in the water, some loose timber and weeping families gathered at the site. The bodies of the dead are still entombed underneath the Michigamme, suspended in a barrage of mud, ore and water.

Counts of those killed fluctuated in newspapers as the rescue efforts continued over the next few days. The *Spokane Daily Chronicle* declared forty-five deceased. The *Daily Advocate* in Ohio said forty dead. The *Aurora Daily Express* and the *Kendallville Standard* both reported twenty-eight. The final count eventually lowered to twenty-seven, and that number has been seared into history in the communities surrounding the former mine.

After the cave-in, Mansfield essentially became a ghost town. What wasn't destroyed in the resolve of the residents took another hit the next year when a forest fire leveled nearly everything. In the early 1900s, the town was rebuilt, the river was rerouted and a new mine opened under the Oliver Iron Mining Company. That ran until 1913, when the supply of iron ore was exhausted. Again the mine closed, but this time it never reopened. Residents left, and Mansfield ceased to exist. All that remains of the town today is some crumbling homes, a restored church, a memorial plaque listing the names of the dead at the location of the cave-in and, perhaps, the ghostly forms of twenty-seven miners who continue to haunt passersby.

Barbara Hahn and her husband, visitors to the memorial site, saw firsthand the remains of the miners' spirits. During a trip to the site by the river, they heard pickaxes hitting rocks, followed by some disembodied screams. At the water's edge, they watched twenty-seven points of light shine up from the depths and quietly disappear again—one light for each of the miners lost. Locals also see the lights, along with apparitions of miners walking to and from their job. They also frequently report hearing screams of the men as they relive in death the tragedy of their lives being snuffed out.

What mineshafts didn't collapse or cave in were mostly left open and abandoned across the Upper Peninsula, becoming hazards for both locals and visitors who could accidentally fall in to their deaths. One such incident happened in Calumet.

The Tamarack Mine opened in 1882 as the brainchild of John Daniell, the superintendent of the Osceola Mine. Osceola had not been profitable, and Daniell spent his time trying to find a new way to make money from the

Calumet in the heyday of mining operations. *Library of Congress.*

copper deep beneath the surface. Eventually, he had a stroke of genius—and perhaps lunacy. Daniell knew that copper streaked through the earth at a downward angle, so in his attempt to find it, he decided to dig mine shafts that went straight down. He figured that eventually, he'd have to hit the copper he had a hunch was right below his feet.

Daniell was right. The Tamarack Mine dropped five shafts down into the earth, each stretching to about a mile long. Five years after the mine formed, the company was making a profit from the copper the shafts ran into—and they ran into a lot of it. Tamarack continued making a profit for the next thirty-five years, producing more than 389 million pounds of copper and becoming the second-most profitable mine in the region.

The Tamarack No. 4 Shaft was completely vertical, stretching about 4,400 feet down into the ground and measuring 12 feet by 18 feet wide. The shaft was mined until 1931, when it was left abandoned and open. A concrete plug installed in 1936 stopped the shaft's descent at about 1,100 feet, and the hole was capped with a concrete slab. That block of concrete, though, did nothing to stop the fate of poor Ruth Ann Miller.

Thirty years after the shaft was closed off, seven-year-old Ruth Ann was out playing with her ten-year-old brother, Gary, and one of their friends. She was playing hide-and-seek and managed to slip through a hole in the barbed wire fence that surrounded the mineshaft. Ruth Ann climbed on top of the shaft's cap, which was badly eroded from thirty years of neglect. After one joyful shout to her brother and friend of "You can't find me!" she fell through a crack in the cap and down about eight hundred feet to her death in the mineshaft.

Rescue efforts began immediately. It was morning on July 16 when she fell in, and the fire department arrived around noon, complete with equipment to take the men down into the shaft. The first to descend was Calumet and Hecla fire chief Al Beauchene, who used a ladder to go down a bit and shout out Ruth Ann's name, hoping she might still be alive and able to call for help. The rescue team realized with Beauchene's descent that the hole was too narrow to effectively get down, and the concrete cap over the shaft would have to be removed.

Removing the cap proved trickier than the rescuers expected though. As it was being lifted, part of it broke off and fell down the shaft to meet Ruth Ann. This didn't deter rescue efforts. They continued for three days. Two mine captains, Joseph Weiss and William Langdon, took a caged mine car down into the shaft, again shouting out for Ruth Ann and listening intently for a response.

Executives for the Calumet and Hecla mining company came to the rescue site to lend their knowledge of the inner workings of the mine. Burton C. Peterson, the president and general manager of the Calumet Division, stayed at the site for the entire three days, getting updates from the men going down into the mine. Vice-President of Administration Jack Gaffney flew in from Chicago to meet Ralph Sanford, the director of employee and public relations.

The rescue operation was incredibly hazardous, and the dedicated company men stayed to see it through. In the end, though, it was all for naught. The team eventually discovered that the portion of the cap that fell into the mine got lodged at about five hundred feet and created a barrier impossible to get past. Little Ruth Ann was sealed into the mineshaft forever.

That mineshaft has since been transformed into a grave site and memorial for Ruth Ann. It's been completely sealed over with concrete, and a chain-link fence surrounds the spot where she fell in. Flowers and stuffed animals consistently show up at the site, placed there by family members, old friends or just curious passersby. Her epitaph hangs on a plaque from the gate:

> *Your life's brief journey ended*
> *At the deep and lonely mine*
> *But oh little Ruth Ann Miller*
> *It is now a cherished shrine*

In 1988, Ruth Ann's mother joined her in death, having her life's wish fulfilled of being interred at the same site where she lost her darling daughter.

The aftermath of the young girl's death did lead to change in the Copper Country, though, in the form of stricter regulations and rules about capping off abandoned mineshafts throughout the region. It also led to some changes of the spookier kind. Locals and guests experience a bevy of supernatural occurrences at the site. Some report ghostly shadows or the patter of little feet behind them. But most heartening are the reports of a child's laughter rising up from the shaft, showing that even in death, Ruth Ann has happily continued her joyous game of hide-and-seek with her brother and friend.

ON THE WATER

In 1866, the Ontonagon Lighthouse began its service. The yellow brick building sits at the mouth of the Ontonagon River, jutting about a quarter mile into Lake Superior. It's a small but stately structure, watching over the ships that pass through the Ontonagon piers and out into the Gitche Gumee. According to the Ontonagon County Historical Society, eleven lighthouse keepers lived in the building with their families over the nearly one hundred years the light was in service. But some of them, it seems, refused to abandon their post after death.

When the light started operations in 1866, Irishman Tom Stripe took on the task of running the house. He was a small man, with a wife and children who lived across the river and didn't move into the lighthouse home. Stripe was left on his own to handle both duties of light and house, carrying up fuel every night to ignite the lantern in the tower. But poor Tom had it a bit more difficult than most: an accident left him without the lower half of his right arm.

Still, though, he persisted. His job as light tender involved carrying a heavy five-gallon oil can up the winding staircase to the lantern room. At first, the

Former light keeper Tom Stripe haunts the Ontonagon Lighthouse. *Michigan Technological University Archives and Copper Country Historical Collections.*

can would be filled with whale oil, but later Stripe would use kerosene. The only thing is, kerosene burned quick. Every four hours, Tom had to head upstairs to refill the lantern's tank.

Moving up the stairs with the oil can was a particular challenge for Stripe. With only one hand, he had to choose between carrying the can and keeping his hand on the bannister for balance. The oil can won every time. But it was heavy, so Stripe often took breaks on the climb up the stairs to put the can down and rest. Once he got into the lantern room, he had to hoist the can onto his shoulder in order to fill the light's tank. Stripe repeated this process, night after night, hours after hours, until he was relieved of duty in 1883.

But though Tom went home to his family across the river, in death his spirit remains in that tower, continuing his walk up and down the stairs with the old oil can. The can is now on display in the lower hall, but it doesn't always want to stay there. Visitors to the lighthouse at night will hear it, the loud *clang* of a metal can being set down on the steps, over and over, as Tom takes his short rests while heading upstairs.

On one particular winter evening, one of the lighthouse guides was up in the tower at night making sure that Christmas lights were hung properly. Suddenly the guide heard it—*clank, clank, clank*—the sound of the oil can coming up the stairs in Stripe's faithful routine. It would have been easy enough to ignore, except for one thing. When the guide turned to head back down, the oil can had mysteriously moved from its location in the lower hall and ended up right there on the second staircase landing.

Yet another time, the oil can made an appearance, although this instance was slightly more menacing. A guide was leading a tour through the lighthouse, but when the group attempted to go up the stairs to the second floor, it was stopped in its tracks. Not by anything visible, of course, but by a solid, cold, invisible barrier. Whatever was in the tower stairwell refused to let the guide up; the group physically could not push past the frozen blockade. After a minute or so, the regular clanking of Stripe's climb up the tower began. Once the noise stopped, the guide was finally able to move forward with the tour. The Ontonagon County Historical Society says this was the only time Stripe's spirit has caused spectral mayhem in the daylight; every other appearance is late at night.

Stripe isn't the only ghost haunting the Ontonagon Lighthouse though. On stormy nights, voices ring out throughout the building, both of adults and children. Most often, they speak of the weather and the wind. It's said that these ghostly voices can even predict storms, preparing to warn the sailors of impending danger even in death. Often, lamps and pieces of furniture will relocate to different places in the night, and beds that were made mysteriously become unkempt. And at least one ghost wants to help the historical society guides—the windows in the tower hardly ever need to be cleaned because some invisible hand has already done the job.

At least one entire ephemeral family remains to protect the lighthouse from danger. On August 25, 1896, all of Ontonagon was destroyed in a fire, with the exception of the lighthouse. A brush fire started nearby the town and was pushed on by a strong wind, destroying the Diamond Match Company's mill and yard close to the lighthouse. But thanks to the perseverance of light keeper James Corgan and his family, the lighthouse survived.

The group of four (Corgan, his wife, their daughter and a hired girl) ran up and down the tower steps, over and over, carrying up buckets of water gathered from the river. Once at the top, they'd throw the water out the tower windows onto the lighthouse building below to keep it from catching fire. They went on in this manner for hours, fighting through heavy smoke and sand that burned their feet until, finally, the wind shifted. The fire changed course, burning Ontonagon but sparing the lighthouse they toiled to save.

That August 25 was a Tuesday, and to this day, every year when August 25 falls on a Tuesday, onlookers can see the scene once again—just in shadowy form. Nothing appears on the lighthouse itself, but when the setting sun projects shadows onto the lawn, silhouettes run through the windows, carrying pail after pail of water to the top of the tower and throwing them onto the roof below.

Fire plays another role in hauntings at the lighthouse, although these are concentrated on the expanse of water just outside. In July 1885, a fire from an unknown source overtook the tugboat *Thomas Quayle*, burning it down to the waterline as it sat moored at the lighthouse dock. The tug continues to burn today, though only reflected in the lighthouse's windows. On the side facing the river, the bright-orange glow of a ghostly fire brightens the glass, and onlookers from the opposite banks can see the fire flickering in reflection.

Before the *Thomas Quayle* was lost, another ship became the victim of a deadly fire. The *St. Clair*, a passenger ship and freighter, left Ontonagon about midnight on July 8, 1876. Fourteen miles later, the ship caught fire. The vessel was carrying a full load of passengers and a deck full of livestock in addition to the crew. It never made it past Fourteen-Mile Point. The captain, Robert Rhynas, tried in vain to beach the ship so everyone could escape, but it never made it. Only five people survived the sinking: Captain Rhynas, first engineer Daniel Stringer, first mate Thomas Boothman, wheelman Thomas

Fortier and passenger John Sutphan. The rest on board perished in the waters off Fourteen-Mile Point, reliving their death every year on the July 8 anniversary, when those looking east from the lighthouse tower can see the flicker of flame once again.

While the haunted Ontonagon Lighthouse is no longer in operation, another haunted lighthouse still warns ships of rocky shoals and potential danger: the Eagle Harbor Lighthouse. A light has been at this spot, the rocky entrance to Eagle Harbor in the Keweenaw Peninsula, since 1851, although the current light station replaced the original in 1871. Three main buildings compose the site: the lighthouse itself, a white house and a brown house. When light keepers still lived on-site, the station was watched over by a head keeper and two assistants. When the light became automated in 1990, the complex turned into a historical society and museum. The lighthouse is still operational, though, so no one is allowed to go up in the tower.

The entrance to Eagle Harbor has always been a particularly dangerous path into the Keweenaw. The shoreline is jagged, and rocks jut up from the lakebed unseen under Lake Superior's often roiling waves. The potential for shipwrecks and the associated loss of life is high here. But surprisingly, it's not the water or shoreline that's haunted—it's two of the buildings in the lighthouse complex, and many who have visited or stayed there have never returned for fear of the ghosts.

One visitor to the site recounted walking into an old bedroom in the lighthouse when, suddenly, a cradle in the room began to shake uncontrollably. He said it was rocking wildly, practically jumping off the floor. No one was near the cradle. As he stared, some more guests came and asked him why the cradle was rocking. He told them it started on its own; the other visitors left immediately and refused to come back in the room.

Perhaps the spookiest story at the lighthouse, though, is the account of an anonymous Coast Guard officer who lived at the light station in the 1970s. He relayed his tale to the *Upper Peninsula Traveler*, a local tourism publication:

> *I enlisted in the Coast Guard on Nov. 3, 1975, and was transferred to Light Station Eagle Harbor in Jan., 1976, where I spent three years....I lived a year in the lighthouse, a year in the big white house, and a year in the short brown house.*
>
> *At the time, the lighthouse and the white house were heavily haunted. The brown house was fine. But shortly after I moved into the lighthouse, strange noises would come from the bedroom on the second floor, like furniture was being dragged heavily across the floor, with sounds of loud footsteps. The*

The Eagle Harbor Lighthouse continually terrified residents of the light station. *Library of Congress.*

light switch at the bottom of the tower would mysteriously click on and off continually. I could see the light coming on from under the door to the tower on the main floor. When I would open the door and look down, it would stop, until I closed the door. My alarm clock would be in a different spot in the morning, or turned off in the night.

I was constantly calling the Coast Guard District Office in Cleveland, complaining that the lighthouse was haunted and I wanted a transfer, and they just shrugged it off.

35

A guest once claimed to have seen a ghost in the bedroom late at night, a man in a plaid flannel shirt with no face. The next morning, she left the lighthouse in extreme fear, and never came back.

After tolerating this for a year, the white house became vacant, and I anxiously moved in. This house turned out to be worse. I would be awakened in the middle of the night, especially in winter, by voices in the bedroom. Footsteps would be heard downstairs late at night on the hardwood floors. They would then slowly come upstairs, down the hall, and stop at the entrance of the master bedroom. By this time, I would be absolutely terrified, laying in bed covered in sweat. The footsteps would start again on the ceiling a few minutes later. Strange things and noises would happen almost continuously.

A year later, a vacancy came up for the brown house, and I moved in. In this house, I never heard or experienced anything strange at all. Probably a good thing, or I would have gone completely nuts. I was stationed there so long, many other families would come and go. Everyone who lived in the white house and the lighthouse were terrified of the hauntings.

Only two known deaths occurred at the Eagle Harbor Lighthouse: keeper James Bouden, who died about seven months into his tenure there, and keeper Stephen Cocking, who stayed on for twelve years before passing in the lighthouse from pneumonia. Perhaps one day the ghosts will let us know which ones they are.

Ghosts have appeared in an even more unlikely place near the Keweenaw Peninsula: underwater. The steamer ship *Emperor*'s wreck graces the waters at Isle Royale's Canoe Rocks. On June 3, 1947, the *Emperor* came powering out of Thunder Bay, carrying a load of ten thousand tons of iron ore. First mate James Morrey took over the watch at midnight, but he had also been responsible for ensuring the ship was loaded with all the iron and he was dead tired. Morrey's fatigue kept him from making regular navigational checks, and a new helmsman who wasn't familiar with that part of the lake didn't consider that when the ship turned left, the boat might possibly run headfirst into Canoe Rocks. This is exactly what it did. Within thirty minutes, the ship had sunk, taking twelve of the crew with it, including Morrey.

The *Emperor* remains in that spot, the bough 20 feet underwater and the stern down at 150 feet. It's relatively intact—the ship hasn't collapsed on itself like other wrecks in the Lakes tend to do. At least one of the crew remains intact as well. One diver exploring the shipwreck swam into the

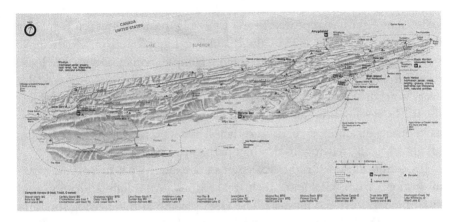

A map of Isle Royale, where many ships ran aground, suffering great loss of life.

stern cabin. Some of the bunks are still upright because of the way the ship sank. As the diver entered the room and looked around, she saw a man lying on one of the bunks. No protection, no diving gear—just someone lying there. She looked at him, and he turned his head and looked at her. The two stared at each other for a moment before she turned and left, leaving the wreck completely. At that same wreck, another diver heard the ghostly sounds of the steam engine thumping its way to life, with no other boats in the vicinity to cause the noise.

Paulding Light: Debunked

On a dark night more than fifty years ago, a railway brakeman faced a problem. Several railcars were stalled on the railroad tracks, and another train was heading right to the spot. He knew that the engineer of the oncoming train needed to be warned in order to avoid a major accident. So the brakeman hopped off the train and waved a lit lantern back and forth along the tracks, hoping to catch the engineer's attention. The poor brakeman never stood a chance. The engineer never saw him, and as the train slammed into the stalled cars, the brakeman was caught in between and crushed to death.

In 1966, a group of students gathered in the night at dead-end Robbins Pond Road in Paulding. What they saw pushed them to go right to the sheriff: a ghostly light floating over the exact spot where our poor brakeman was killed. The light has appeared nearly every night since with such regularity that it's now officially named the "Paulding Light," and hundreds make regular pilgrimages to the spot to catch a glimpse. Sometimes it's one light, sometimes two, and sometimes the color changes to red, white or green. But every time, the light mimics the path of the brakeman walking up and down the tracks, getting brighter as it comes closer and then fading into darkness as he meets his untimely end. And then it starts over again as he continues his ghostly walk, reliving his death in perpetuity.

It's a fantastic story, right? Except it's not exactly true. In 2010, a group of students from Michigan Tech trekked out to the light's location and attempted to solve the mystery. They set up camp at the viewing spot and waited for the light to appear, which it did—because it *always* does. With step one complete, they left and returned another day with a telescope. When the light appeared again, they peered through the scope and found the lights coming from an everyday source: cars driving down a highway—a highway that was coincidentally built in 1966. They didn't stop their investigation there, though. The group wanted the mystery truly and thoroughly debunked. So they sent team member Bill Norkus out to the specific spot on the highway they could see through the telescope (which was easy enough to find thanks to an Adopt-a-Highway sign). Norkus logged every car that went by, and the rest of the team logged every instance of seeing the Paulding Light. The reports matched perfectly. Every time a car drove by, the light appeared. To further test the theory, Norkus drove down the highway himself with his hazards on, and sure enough, the team saw a flashing yellow Paulding Light. Unfortunately, it seems that the light is far more terrestrial than everyone wanted to believe.

But that doesn't stop people from visiting the spot on a regular basis. Paranormal purists think that the Michigan Tech report is bunk, and the hopeful continue to sit and wait at the edge of the woods to see the soft glow of a lost railroader's lantern…or the spark of a local Native American ghost's dance atop the power lines…or a grandparent with a faulty lantern looking for a missing grandchild…or something even spookier. On a Paulding pilgrimage, the possibilities are endless.

PART II
CENTRAL PENINSULA GHOSTS

HOTEL AND BUSINESS HAUNTS

Iron mines and logging outfits dominate the central Upper Peninsula. Three iron ranges run through the UP, and in the mid-1800s, geologists mapped them out to near perfection. In 1846, the first small but profitable amounts of iron ore began to ship. The industry struggled until 1884, when the railroad came through, bringing with it a flood of workers from all over the world who wanted to make a living off iron.

If immigrants coming over from Europe chose not to go to the mines, they generally went into the logging business. Logging in the Upper Peninsula began with the French fur traders so they could build their forts, trading posts and missions. Eventually, the settlements they put down turned into lumber camps in the early 1800s, and the industry spread across the UP, quickly overcoming the fur trade as the main source of income for residents—which now included Americans and large immigrant communities. An elaborate system of winding rivers throughout the region helped business, allowing lumber companies to quickly get logs to the mills and their customers.

Nahma is one such logging town. A water-powered sawmill popped up on the nearby Sturgeon River in 1848. By 1856, a town had emerged close by, and the residents got their first post office. Five years later, Delta County (Nahma's home) was organized, with Nahma Township being the first to reside within the county borders. A county road came through in 1868, followed by a highway the next year.

Although it had humble beginnings, Nahma really began to take off in 1881, when the Bay de Noquet Lumber Company opened. Soon, 1,200 men were working at the company, and more than 800 of those employees lived in Nahma. The St. Lawrence Catholic Church provided spiritual guidance for locals, with services once a month when the priest came in by train from Sault Ste. Marie.

Bay de Noquet was the hub of old Nahma. It provided workers and their families with a clubhouse containing sports facilities, a soda fountain, a library, a barbershop and a few lounges and bars. Nearby, the company ran a golf course, provided land for hunting, hosted a public beach and built a network of sidewalks and trails. Several more churches opened in the early 1900s, along with a community hall. The town continued to flourish until 1951, when the lumber company shut down due to a lack of available timber.

The population in Nahma tanked, and shortly after Bay de Noquet closed, the entire town was sold to an Indiana company called American Playground. The ultimate goal was to turn Nahma into a resort, but (perhaps fortunately) the company's owner lacked the necessary funds to make the conversion. By 1994, so much of the land had been sold off that only fifteen acres of Nahma remained. At that point, the Groleau family purchased the land, and the town—now only containing a store, an office, a beach, a hotel and a school—set about preserving what was left. Today, the town of Nahma itself has a population of about fifty-nine, with fewer than five hundred remaining in the entire township.

The Nahma Inn (which was the remaining hotel in the Groleaus' purchase) carries the history of old Nahma. It was built in 1909 as a hotel for Bay de Noquet employees. One of the frequent guests was Charlie Good, once president of the lumber company. He became infatuated with a kitchen worker at the inn, Nell Fleming, and they soon fell headfirst into an affair. Miss Nell, as she was known, deeply loved Good. One day, though, he left and never returned. In her anguish at losing her love, Miss Nell retreated to a room on the second floor, keeping watch outside in the hopes that one day he might return.

Nell remains at that window today, often seen by visitors looking up to the second floor, where she can be seen sitting, still waiting for her lost love. But she doesn't spend her entire existence at that window. Nell often moves about the house, and guests have reported seeing her apparition both in the kitchen and heading upstairs to resume her post. In the kitchen, she has a tendency to clean and reorganize, spelling confusion for the staff coming in the next morning who don't know where anything is anymore.

In her room, Nell likes to tidy up as well—guests frequently find that the bed has moved sometime during the day, and their belongings have ended up in new spots. Trish Kautz, one of the Yooper Paranormal Investigators team, said that her phone was mysteriously moved into an equipment case from the nightstand, and a friend's recording equipment wound up on the other side of the room from where she placed it. It may well be a prank by Nell; the investigators once caught a woman laughing after a particularly active session. The lights in Nell's room also turn on and off by themselves.

Miss Nell is joined by a number of other spirits at the Nahma Inn. Owner Charley MacIntosh thinks that Charlie Good is haunting the second floor as well, as visitors often hear footsteps above them when they're on the first floor. He's also heard an adult singing lullabies, perhaps to the ten-year-old girl his wife and the co-owner, Laurie, have seen on multiple occasions. Employees at the inn hear ghostly voices in mid-conversation and have watched coins randomly fall from the ceiling and knives sporadically be pulled off a magnet strip and placed on the floor. Once, a guest even reported a whole lounge full of ghosts—he could hear a rollicking party downstairs from his room, but when he went to check it out, the lounge was completely empty and the lights were off. When he went back upstairs, he couldn't shake the feeling that he was being watched, which lasted all night and into the next day.

But although most of the resident spirits at Nahma are said to be friendly, if not a little heartbroken or bored, some appear to be downright crabby. Another Yooper Paranormal investigator, Kelly Carlson, once recorded a voice in one of the rooms telling them, "Keep out," but she didn't think there was anything malicious about it—instead, it's just a grumpy ghost that wants some time alone.

But others aren't quite as convinced. One claims to have been eating lunch at the Nahma Inn when a feisty ghost heard them talking about Nell. In response, a spoon flew across the dining room and hit the diner's mother in the elbow. Everyone else at the table still had their spoons. The owner himself has experienced a slightly more hectic version of the ghosts. One Thanksgiving, Charley and three friends were playing euchre and having drinks. Apparently, one of the drinks didn't satisfy the thirsty ghost, and the glass flung itself off the table.

The Landmark Inn in historic Marquette, the Upper Peninsula's largest town, shares a trait with the Nahma Inn: a bevy of ghosts haunting the hotel.

Marquette has always been one of the largest cities in the Upper Peninsula; today, it is the biggest. *Library of Congress.*

Marquette was built on the backs of the iron miners, with gigantic ore docks jutting out into the lake. These docks attached to the railroad. Train cars bringing in iron pellets from the west would climb up the docks and dump their load into waiting freighters, which would then start their haul across the Great Lakes.

Marquette was already a bustling town when the Landmark Inn opened. It began its life as the Northland Hotel, with an exceptionally long opening process. The idea to build the hotel arose in 1910. The foundation finally started to take shape in 1917, but it would be another thirteen years before visitors arrived. The Northland Hotel finally opened on January 8, 1930, with one hundred rooms.

For nearly the next forty years, the hotel was the place to be and be seen in Marquette. Almost every celebrity heading through town stayed there— including Amelia Earhart, Abbott and Costello, Louis Armstrong, Duke Ellington and even the members of the Rolling Stones. The Northland Hotel was the home base for the cast and crew of *Anatomy of a Murder*, and during the

Formerly the Northland Hotel, the Landmark Inn was a beacon for celebrities and socialites. *Author's collection.*

1959 filming, Jimmy Stewart himself graced the halls. Both American and foreign presidents and dignitaries have stayed at the hotel.

Nearing the late 1970s, though, the Northland Hotel fell on hard times. Revenue was down, and repairs needed were up. The hotel became a victim of financial hardship and ended up in disrepair, finally closing in 1982. It languished for another thirteen years, until it was bought and completely restored in 1995. The property rebranded as the Landmark Hotel, paying homage to the building's history as an iconic Marquette property. The hotel is once again a famous lodging spot in the Upper Peninsula—the Rolling Stones even came back in 2002—but some of the inn's past never left it. The Landmark Inn is considered one of the most haunted hotels in Michigan.

In the mid-1900s, before construction on the Northland Hotel was even complete, the first ghostly legend came to life—or rather, death. Thanks to financing problems, it took thirteen years to complete construction on the building. During the process, the unfinished hotel was a regular haunt for men working on business negotiations and for ladies of the night to entertain those men. They'd wander the empty halls and stay in the unfinished rooms, getting their fill of both whiskey and women. One of the female escorts, though, got into a bit of trouble. One story says she wasn't being faithful to the customer who loved her; in another, she was sharing deal secrets with other patrons in some light pillow talk. But both stories end the same way: the escort was murdered by one of the businessmen in a drunken fit of rage. Terrified of the consequences he might face, the man acted quickly. He took the body down to the unfinished basement and buried her there, letting the construction crew continue to raise the building around her.

She didn't go without a fight though. Throughout the rest of the construction process, workers often reported crying and a terrifyingly quiet whisper of a woman, urging them closer and closer to her burial spot, in hopes that they might uncover her body and the heinous crime that occurred.

The Landmark Inn's other main haunting was born out of love. When the hotel first opened in the 1930s, iron ore ships would constantly come in and out of the harbor. One sailor got to know the town and often stayed at the Northland Hotel during his visits. He'd also make pilgrimages to the local library every time his ship brought him to Marquette. It was here that he fell madly in love with a librarian. The two frequently met at the hotel during his trips, and as the relationship progressed, they made plans to marry and settle in the town. The librarian's love had just one more sail before he could quit—long enough to allow his employer to find a replacement. He left her on his final trip with hope in her heart and an expectation that they would wed when he returned. But when she went to meet him in their regular room at the hotel, he never arrived. The poor sailor had fallen victim to a ghastly Lake Superior storm and perished on the ocean floor with the entire ship's crew. The librarian was never able to recover. She watched out the window of their room at the hotel waiting for him for as long as she could stand it, and in her heartbreak, she hanged herself in that very room.

Today, the sixth-floor room is known as the Lilac Room. It's said the librarian loved lilacs—she wore a lilac print, and lilacs grace the wallpaper in her hotel room. When renovations on the hotel were completed, the librarian appeared again. Guests report a woman in a lilac-patterned dress wandering the halls of the sixth floor, and she's even been spotted in the bar on that floor, examining the fabric of a guest's lilac-patterned skirt. But most of the activity happens in the Lilac Room itself. Visitors have reported hearing a crying woman close to the window, objects moving by themselves and furnishings looking used after the room has been empty. The first guest

The ghost of a lovesick librarian haunts the halls of the Landmark Inn. *Author's collection.*

who stayed in the Lilac Room after the renovations had a unique problem with the librarian's ghost. He found screws between his sheets, and when he called to have them removed, they appeared again later in the day, even after multiple checks by housekeeping staff. The librarian herself often calls down to the front desk, prompting many reports of calls coming from the room while it's vacant and eerie silence on the other end of the line. She's probably checking in vain to see if her lost love has arrived yet from his fateful trip. In her anguish, she also has a tendency to keep out male guests; men staying in the room frequently report trouble with their room keys, only to have the room easily open when a female employee tries the same key.

Down on the southern side of the Upper Peninsula and closer to Nahma, the port city of Escanaba has its own set of feisty ghosts haunting another hotel, the House of Ludington. The first white settlers came to Escanaba in 1830. The head of the group was a fur trader named Louis Roberts, who came to love the river Native Americans had used for centuries as a plentiful fishing spot. More settlers followed, and the first sawmill burst into operation, attracting a surveyor named Eli Royce. He platted the original town of Escanaba, naming it Escanawba after the local native word for the place. It translates to "flat rock." The city was officially organized in 1863. Eventually the *w* in the name was dropped, and as more residents came, it grew into a bustling town of loggers, fishers, paper mill workers and iron miners.

The House of Ludington opened in 1865 as the Gaynor House Hotel. It ran until 1883, when it switched hands, was torn down and rebuilt and reopened as a new business, the New Ludington Hotel. The owner then, John Christie, oversaw hotel expansion to end up with one hundred rooms. The building again changed hands in 1939, purchased by Chicago mob-connected Pat Hayes. As owner, Hayes worked as host, chef and manager of the property, but he also had an eccentric temper that made its way into the business. He refused to serve anyone a well-done steak in the restaurant, and when it was requested, that person got fish or chicken or a swift kick out the door. Hayes also fought with city officials to install Michigan's first glass elevator, which he added in 1959. Apparently, the argument got so heated that Hayes threatened to sit outside the hotel with a shotgun during the elevator's construction and shoot anybody who tried to interfere. There are rumors that Hayes, a friend of Al Capone's, used the hotel's three basements (and the connected tunnels) to store illegal mob hooch, which is potentially still buried beneath the building. In 1969, Hayes died of prostate cancer while in the hotel.

Chicago mob–connected Pat Hayes once owned the House of Ludington Hotel…and never left.

Since 1998, Suzell and Ed Eisenberger have owned the hotel, and they maintain that Hayes still haunts the building. The glass elevator (which still works) has a tendency to run up and down on its own, over and over again. Perhaps Hayes is the resident ghost that reeks of tobacco and body odor and generally has a crabby energy. It's been reported that in the room where he died, guests often feel a presence sit down on the end of their bed.

In addition to Hayes's ghostly presence, nearly every owner of the building has reported phantom steps creaking up the staircase at exactly 5:15 a.m. every morning. Rocking chairs rock on their own, and furniture constantly rearranges itself. And one of the resident ghosts appears to have the Christmas spirit every year—the angel always finds a way to the top of the tree without help from anyone living. As of this writing, the House of Ludington was in the process of being sold and converted to apartments.

Other haunted businesses in the central Upper Peninsula focus on Marquette. The Chocolay River Trading Post furniture store, for example, was at one point both a furniture store and a morgue. The owners of the store (it was called Oakley's then) kept bodies from winter deaths preserved in the basement until the thaw, when it was possible to bury them in the previously frozen earth. Employees of the store now still hesitate to go into the basement, thanks to creepy feelings and vibes left from all the corpses.

The *Marquette Monthly* office has a particularly colorful story. Supposedly, there was once a small printing press on the top floor of the building before the periodical arrived. Beth Ann, who owned the house with her husband, was responsible for running the press upstairs. One night, the story goes, Beth Ann's sleeve got caught in the press. The machine slowly ripped her arm off, her tortured cries heard by only the empty house. When her husband arrived home from work, he found his poor mangled wife on the floor, missing an arm and lying in a pool of her own blood. According to this story, *Marquette Monthly* employees can still hear Beth Ann screaming for help from the top floor of the office.

But like the story of the Paulding Light ghost, this, too, has been thoroughly debunked. A previous employee of the *Monthly* traced back ownership of the building and found that it had been a grocery store and a gift shop before the magazine purchased it, but it never did have a printing press up top. Coincidentally, though, the building does appear to be haunted by a different ghost: Ray LaBonte, a descendant of the building's grocery store owner. LaBonte's ghost is mostly playful or restless, hiding important things, throwing items around the room, pacing upstairs or messing with the electricity.

A GHOSTLY COLLEGE

In 1899, a new school opened in Marquette. It was called the Northern State Normal School, located on twenty-two sprawling acres (donated by John Longyear, a local businessman), where thirty-two students hoping to become teachers attended, under the tutelage of six professors. The teachers trained here would then be shipped across the Upper Peninsula to work at schools in the lesser-populated regions.

The school went through several iterations over the next sixty years. Enrollment increased annually, and the school's name changed along with the incoming students. In 1927, it became the Northern State Teachers College. In 1942, it became the Northern Michigan College of Education. In 1955, the name was changed to Northern Michigan College. Two years later, the Mackinac Bridge opened, and with that, enrollment swelled and the college transformed yet again. A new state constitution in 1963 gave the

NORTHERN STATE NORMAL SCHOOL, MARQUETTE.

NOTE.—The above engraving represents the completed building as planned, with the $25,000 appropriated by the Legislature of 1899, and the assistance of Marquette citizens, the south wing only has been built.

This engraving shows the planned Northern State Normal School in Marquette before construction.

The Northern State Normal School as it looked six years after construction, in 1905.

school official university status, and it became formally known by today's name: Northern Michigan University. Now, the school has 177 degree programs and about 7,900 students.

And those are just the living attendees. A full slate of ghosts haunts NMU's hallowed halls. The most well known is that of the former friendly janitor, Perry. Perry Fezatt was a local Marquette resident and former World War II paratrooper when he came to work as a janitor at Northern Michigan University. He had been married and was expecting a child, but both his wife and child died in birth a few years following their marriage. Afterward, he moved in with his aging mother, although his ultimate plan was to retire and move out to his camp down near the Wisconsin border.

Poor Perry would never make it to camp though. He was only five-foot-seven yet weighed about three hundred pounds. He had multiple health conditions, including heart concerns that he managed with medication. On April 12, 1983, according to coworker Mike McKinney, who worked with him throughout the '70s, and Fezatt's death certificate, Perry had a heart attack and died in the elevator in the service hall connecting the Thomas Fine Arts Building and the Forest Roberts Theatre. Most reports say that he passed on a Friday and wasn't found until the following Monday, but his death certificate shows that he died on a Tuesday—a student or other employee likely found him that same day. He was fifty-seven years old.

Supposedly, Perry never left those buildings. During his life, McKinney said, Perry often spent time in the Forest Roberts Theatre. He enjoyed watching the rehearsals and productions and became friends with the head of the theater department, Dr. James Rapport. To this day, actors waiting for their turn to go on stage have sensed a jovial presence or felt a ghostly hand on their shoulders.

He's been seen throughout both the theater and the fine arts building, though most frequently coming out of the elevator in the basement. One person reported seeing him carrying a mop and smiling by the elevator, while others have seen him walking around both buildings or continuing about his work in the afterlife. But most interactions with Perry's ghost are from something unseen, causing a cold draft or the feeling of someone else in the room when no one is there.

The elevator itself often reacts to Perry's ghostly appearance. Cameras in the building have recorded all sorts of activity after hours, including the doors opening and closing on their own, buttons and service lights going on and the elevator changing floors at random. Sometimes, during the day, the elevator doesn't move at all; it just makes weird mechanical rumblings

The Academic Mall is a central area that connects several buildings at Northern Michigan University.

and stays in place. Or it goes the opposite direction of whichever button has been pushed. Those who knew him described Perry as a practical joker, so while it could just be mechanical issues with the aging elevator, many attribute the tricks to the former janitor, playing pranks on those who still walk the halls.

John X. Jamrich Hall, an office and classroom building with multiple lecture halls on the Northern Michigan campus, is also rumored to be haunted, although these claims are harder to prove. The old building on this spot was torn down and replaced in 2014, and some say that the ghosts left with the remnants of Old Jamrich. The main story from the previous iteration of the building says that a former nursing student haunted the control room. Once upon a time, graduating nursing students would record their names on the wall in the control room, and one wanted to remain to make sure the wall stayed intact. Several reports emerged of a young woman's shadowy face appearing in the control room window, seen by those outside the room and, at one point, by two students inside the room. Most students, though, never experienced anything in the room, and both a medium and multiple teams of ghost hunters never got the sense that anything paranormal was happening in the building. Some claim that the

The bridge on the left connects Jamrich Hall to other NMU campus buildings.

nursing student took up residence in the new Jamrich building, but very few reports have emerged since the destruction of the old one.

Even more tales of spirits haunt the residence halls on campus. Lee Hall, Gant Hall and Halverson Hall all have had their ghosts. Halverson's spirit resided in room 304, and although the building has since been torn down, her story continues as an urban legend at the school. Supposedly, a young female student hanged herself from the top bunk in her dorm room and never left. She's been seen roaming around the third floor, looking out her window or scraping her nails along the chalkboards in the floor's study rooms. Reports of a suicide in that building don't appear to exist, though, and someone who lived in the same room after the alleged suicide noted that nothing out of the ordinary ever happened.

According to one of the founders of the paranormal research team at Northern Michigan University, though, a suicide *did* happen on campus, just in Gant Hall, not Halverson. But again, no factual evidence to back that up has been found, and only one relatively sketchy website claims that a ghost haunts Gant, which conveniently matches the reports exactly for what people experienced in Halverson. Gant Hall is slated to be demolished and likely will be by the time of this publication, so we'll probably never know if there really was a suicide and what building it happened in. Also, at one point, the college actively discouraged students from discussing suicidal thoughts and tendencies, as exposed in an editorial for *New York Magazine*'s "The Cut" column, to ensure that friends and fellow students wouldn't see a stress-related decline in the quality of their schoolwork. So with both buildings gone and a culture of silencing self-destructive thoughts, it's no wonder firsthand reports of the alleged suicide(s) don't exist.

Interestingly, both of these residence hall haunting reports began to surface in the 1960s, shortly after Michigan State University in East Lansing downstate reported in its school newspaper that women in the dorms didn't feel safe thanks to the Hatchet Man, a supposed serial killer. The Hatchet Man reportedly dressed in women's clothing and slaughtered forty women with a hatchet throughout the Midwest. Some male pranksters at Michigan State decided to scare the girls on campus by dressing up in women's clothing and running around with a hatchet. The panic arrived at Northern Michigan University nearly right away, with girls in the dorms using a complicated system of passwords before they'd let anyone in their rooms. Some reported getting anonymous phone calls in the night and receiving threatening letters signed "Hatch." The rumors took hold in nearly every midwestern college at the time, turning into urban legends—students at the Indiana University Bloomington campus even began to circulate a story of a female student slaughtered by the Hatchet Man in the hall of her dorm. No one was ever actually killed by a hatchet on campus at the time these stories surfaced, but it's possible that fear led to the creation of NMU's suicide and subsequent haunting tales.

The haunting at Lee Hall is only slightly more corroborated than the others, but again not by actual evidence. Rather, this ghost was sensed by a medium investigating the residence hall with a paranormal group in 2012. Once up in the attic of the building, the medium discovered the spirit of a young girl in a dress. Throughout the course of the investigation, they learned that the girl's name was Anna and that she had been an NMU student. In 1980 or 1981, Anna had just been dumped by her boyfriend when she was out on some cliffs in a nearby town. Those cliffs would be the last thing she ever saw—she fell and drowned in the water below. The investigation team couldn't clarify a few pieces of information though. Anna either committed suicide, accidentally fell or someone pushed her, and the medium said Anna refused to say whether or not she was pregnant at the time of her death. The team was also baffled as to why Anna remains at Lee Hall, especially if she died in a fall from the nearby cliffs.

About one mile off campus, the Peter White Public Library may not officially be a part of the university in Marquette, but students often research there just the same. It was founded in 1871 by Peter White himself, a store owner and lawyer. The first iteration of the library contained only his own books and was located in city hall. It quickly outgrew the space, expanding to a collection of ten thousand books by the next year.

The library moved locations several times on the hunt for an appropriate space. From city hall, it opened in the First National Bank Building, and from there, it moved to the Thurber Block (which continued to revolve around books, as it was home to a Book World bookstore until the chain liquidated in 2017). In 1891, Peter White's library consolidated with the local school district's library. Still the collection grew, and by 1895, the Thurber Block space had become overwhelmed. Efforts to build a new, dedicated library building began, spearheaded by White. Thanks to donations from the community, the current library building opened at the corner of Front and Ridge in 1904. The library was constructed from white limestone, designed specifically to stand out from the reddish-brown buildings throughout Marquette at the time. Additions were added in 1958 and 2000.

Reports of the paranormal started flowing as soon as the library opened in its permanent space. Students and visitors have reported books flying off the shelves, ghostly whispers, apparitions, copy machines sputtering to life at night and feelings of being watched. Ghost investigation teams hit a

In 1905, the Peter White Public Library stood out from the reddish-brown buildings of Marquette.

wall with equipment, which mysteriously stops working once a group walks into the building, but when the equipment does work, investigators catch compelling evidence, like conversations and voices directed at the living people in the library.

One standout was a conversation between a medium and a spirit in the women's bathroom upstairs in the newest part of the library. The medium reported that the spirit's name is Charlotte, and she enjoys hanging out in the bathroom just to watch the people come and go. Charlotte wouldn't give her full name or the exact reason she occupied that bathroom, but it's possible the ghost is of Charlotte Peterson, a woman who lived from 1856 to 1936 and worked for Peter White's sister-in-law's nephew. Perhaps she and White shared a love of books, and she didn't want to leave them behind in death. Peterson is buried in Marquette's Park Cemetery.

MYSTERIOUS LIGHTHOUSES

On top of all the other ghosts in the city, Marquette has a haunted lighthouse as well. The Marquette Harbor Lighthouse was first built in 1853, but shoddy construction of the tower and keeper's quarters led to its replacement thirteen years later, in 1866. That lighthouse, though extensively renovated, is the current one standing on the spot.

Reports say that in the early 1900s, a young girl died at the lighthouse, and her ghost haunts the building. However, no solid evidence of such a death exists, even though around that same time, the daughter of the lighthouse keeper fell on the rocks and badly injured herself. Staff at the lighthouse think that this girl is the actual ghost. Former assistant director Taylor Hegler said the girl's name is Jessie and that she is in a dress and always barefoot. Hegler, who had seen the ghost while giving a tour, even described Jessie down to the red hair and green eyes.

Jessie takes on two manifestations, according to people who have witnessed the haunting. One is a sad story: she appears staring out the upper-floor window of the lighthouse, waiting for the return of her lost mother and father. In the other, Jessie remains a happy young girl, skipping across the floor and laughing, playing on the catwalk, gravitating to children and mothers. At one point, Hegler said, Jessie accidentally walked through wet paint and tracked footprints across the floor in the winch room. Those painted footprints can still be seen today.

A young ghost named Jessie reportedly haunts the Marquette Harbor Lighthouse. *Library of Congress.*

About one hundred miles southeast of Marquette, Seul Choix lighthouse guards the entry to Seul Choix Bay in Gulliver, a small harbor once used by Native Americans and fur traders as a safe spot away from the roiling Lake Michigan waters. As word of the abundant whitefish and lake trout in the bay spread, a thriving fishing community grew. The lighthouse was built over a three-year period, from 1892 to 1895, to alert sailors of the sanctuary amid the otherwise rocky and dangerous coast. Originally, according to the Seul Choix Museum, "the project consisted of a tower, family quarters, a steam fog signal and boiler house, stable, boathouse, two docks, two oil houses, brick outhouse, paint shed and a tramway, which was used to transport supplies from the boats up the slope to the light." The keeper's house was expanded in 1925. The lighthouse still operates today, although it's fully automated—thankfully, no light keeper needs to run up and down the stairs every few hours to light the lamp at the top of the tower. But although he's no longer needed, one head light keeper appears to remain on the premises, making his presence known to both volunteers and visitors.

Joseph W. Townshend died in the keeper's quarters at Seul Choix Lighthouse. *Library of Congress.*

Keeper Joseph W. Townshend first took up residence at Seul Choix in 1901. He was a boat captain from Bristol, England, and arrived in Michigan by way of Canada. He worked as the keeper at both Skillagalee and Waugoshance Shoal lighthouses before taking over in Gulliver. Sadly, Seul Choix would be the last lighthouse Townshend would see. He died of tuberculosis in the keeper's quarters in 1910. But Townshend died in the winter, which meant the ground was too frozen for a proper burial. His body was embalmed in the basement, where it lay at rest for several months until relatives could come and see him interred.

In life, Townshend was a heavy cigar smoker. His wife, though, refused to let him smoke inside the house. But it seems that in death, Townshend is determined to defy her. One of the main ghostly experiences people discover is the smell of cigar smoke wafting through the living quarters, the source unknown.

Most reports of the haunting at Seul Choix emerged in the 1990s, when a dining room table was pulled up from storage in the basement and reassembled for display. As a Brit, Townshend would set the table differently from the American style of putting the fork on the left. Unsurprisingly, staff members at the lighthouse often arrive in the morning to find the fork misplaced—either it's across the top of the plate, moved to the right side or set tines facing down the way Townshend used to like it. Sometimes it's even placed across the knife to form a cross. Plus, both the chairs and the place settings are often disturbed. By the staff's count, the table has needed resetting more than one hundred times.

Townshend makes his mark in other areas of the lighthouse complex as well. He's frequently heard walking up and down the tower steps. Old phonograph music tends to resonate throughout the keeper's house. An imprint appears on the bedspread in the bedroom Townshend died in some mornings, as if someone had been sitting on the bed. A Bible in the museum opens and closes on its own. Batteries routinely lose a charge on the property.

The creepiest stories, though, are those from people who have actually seen old Joseph Townshend on the property. Some say he has appeared to them as a ghostly reflection in a bedroom mirror. One man, at the lighthouse to give an estimate for an alarm installation, saw the image of Townshend staring at him from the lighthouse window—*after* he had already made sure the lighthouse was empty and locked. Townshend's apparition has been seen on the property so often that guests tell the gift shop staff that the reenactor on staff is top notch, walking across the yard in a heavy blue coat on his way to the lighthouse.

Aside from the former keeper, staff at Seul Choix say that two young girls haunt the lighthouse as well, and they come in the morning to find toys strewn about in one of the upstairs bedrooms.

Maritime historian Frederick Stonehouse says that Seul Choix's ghostly energy extends farther down the coast. In an interview for this book, he recounted the tale of Goudreau Harbor, a small French fishing village from the 1800s about two miles west of Seul Choix. Only a few houses remain on the site, mostly used for summer cottages since the fishing industry there is long gone. But the summer residents still see specters of former villagers. Stonehouse noted:

> *One family was in their summer home enjoying a wonderful summer evening, and one of the kids looks out the front window and he sees this woman walking down the street. Now, the street is just a dusty towpath, two-track, and he looks at her, points it out to his mother, points her out to*

his father. The father does a double take, runs on outside to see this woman closer, and of course, by the time he gets out, she's gone. Story goes that it was actually the grandmother of that family who had been long dead.

Another story emerged from a two-bedroom ranch house on the corner in Goudreau Harbor. About thirty years ago, a retired husband and wife used this house as their summer home. Every night, they would sit and watch TV, the husband in his recliner on the right and his wife to the left. One night, the couple decided to switch seats, and the wife was finally able to see down the hallway on the opposite side of the recliner. She only lasted a few minutes before jumping up and screaming, asking about spirits in the hall. Her husband, though, had been seeing them for years and knew they posed no harm.

"What she had been seeing was black figures passing through the hall from left side to right side, down the hall and across it, perpendicular," Stonehouse said, noting that the couple sold the house immediately after because the wife couldn't live with the ghosts. "According to the locals, what they had seen were rock spirits. In the early days of the Great Lakes, when you didn't really have reliable water transportation, people walked along trails on the lakeshore. The principal east–west trail that passed northern Lake Michigan coming from Mackinac Island and the Straits of Mackinac going west literally went right through Goudreau Harbor, literally right through the middle of their home. So, it was simply the spirits of these old travelers still continuing down the trail."

Some of the old lighthouses in the Upper Peninsula have taken on the summer cottage feel, complete with ghosts of their own. Big Bay Point Lighthouse in Big Bay is one of them, transformed into a bed-and-breakfast—just with one guest that never leaves.

The light station at Big Bay Point began service in 1896, marking the halfway point between the Keweenaw Portage Entry and Marquette. Freight and passenger ships running along the south side of Lake Superior always passed Big Bay Point, and that stretch along the coast was completely dark, causing many shipwrecks in the years before the lighthouse opened. The keepers' quarters was originally a duplex; the head light keeper and his family lived on one side, and the assistant keeper and his family lived on the other. In the 1920s, an extension for a third keeper was added.

William H. Prior became the first head keeper of the Big Bay light when it opened in 1896. He transferred over from the Stannard Rock Lighthouse, which was twenty-five miles away. Unfortunately for the assistant keepers working under Prior, the man was ornery and had incredibly high expectations. His trouble seemed to begin a little more than a year after he took his post. He received word that his only sister had died, and he had to go to Marquette for the funeral. Prior walked the entire way—about thirty miles there and thirty miles back. He was only gone for a week, and when he returned, it appeared that assistant keeper Ralph Heater had not done his job. Prior wrote about it in his logbook on November 18, 1897:

> *I can not see that the assistant has done any work around the station since I left. He has not the energy to carry him down the hill and if I speak to him about it he makes no answer, but goes on just as if he did not hear me, he is so much under the control of his wife he has not the hart [sic] to do anything. She has annoyed me during the season by hanging around him and hindering him from working, and she is altogether a person totally unfit to be in a place like this as she is discontented and jealous and has succeeded in making life miserable for everyone at this station.*

> *Signed H. WILLIAM PRIOR.*

The logbook entries about Assistant Heater continued in that manner, noting that he refused to work during the closed season and claimed to have a bad back, yet he also managed to walk to and from Marquette without incident, go fishing with no problems and have easy days on which Prior suggested, "It is Sunday, so his back is not lame today."

Assistant Heater and his family left Big Bay in April 1898 when he was transferred to the light at Granite Island, much to the joy of both Prior and Heater. That same month, a new assistant and his family came to the light, assistant keeper George Beamer. Beamer, though, left the next month to volunteer in the military, leaving his wife, Jennie, in charge until his return in August 1898. Much to Prior's chagrin, Beamer returned from the war complaining of a bad back. This assistant also didn't do so well under Prior's leadership, as evidenced by this series of logbook entries ranging from September 19 to November 1, 1898:

> *September 19, 1898:*
> *Asst. Beamer does not take hold of his work as he should. He evidently expects me to work with him whenever he is at work, and if I do not, he leaves the work and does nothing until I get back to him.*

October 1, 1898:
As Mr. Beamer always objects to my questions and resents my interference, and I have passed over his dereliction before and not caring to be constantly making reports unfavorable to him, I have written this for future reference when the Inspector arrives.

October 7, 1898:
When will I get an assistant who will fit the place?

October 27, 1898:
Asst. Beamer complains of being sick and talks of leaving the station to go home to Detroit. He is too high strung for a light keeper's asst, between himself and his wife this season I imagine that I am keeping a Home for the Helpless Poor instead of a U.S. Lighthouse. I and my family having to do the greater part of the work while they receive the pay.

November 1, 1898:
Put Mr. Beamer on board the steamer to go home. Hired my son George E. Prior as Laborer. This Beamer...is without exception the most ungrateful and the meanest man I ever met.

One more assistant keeper came to the lighthouse, William Crisp, although he only stayed from April 23, 1899, to July 11, 1899, when he insisted on resigning and leaving for Marquette immediately, even if that meant he had to walk there. After Crisp's departure, Prior's son George officially took on the assistant keeper duties.

Although Prior now had his son working for him, presumably an assistant he could deal with, the arrangement had a tragic end. George fell on the rocks about a year after starting his work at the lighthouse. He had to be taken to the hospital in Marquette; Prior took him on April 17, 1901, and left him there to heal. Sadly, on June 13, 1901, Prior had to return to Marquette. His son had died from his injuries.

Prior fell into a deep depression after his son passed away. His usually detailed logbook entries became few and far between, with the last reading only "general work," recorded two weeks after his son's death. The next day, June 28, 1901, he disappeared. The story goes that he walked off into the woods carrying a gun and some strychnine, intending to kill himself. When he didn't return by October, his wife and remaining children left the lighthouse and moved to Marquette.

Prior remained missing for seventeen months. The final entry regarding Big Bay's first head keeper was written by James Bergan, Prior's successor, on November 14, 1902: "Mr. Fred Babcock came to the station 12.30 pm. While hunting in the woods one and a half mile south of the station this noon he found a skeleton of a man hanging in a tree. We went to the place and found that the clothing and everything tally with the former keeper of this station who has been missing seventeen months."

According to legend, Prior hasn't left the light station since. The current owners of the Big Bay Lighthouse Bed-and-Breakfast usually claim that the haunting was a publicity stunt by previous owners, but past visitors have reported seeing an elderly man with a thick mustache and dressed in a Coast Guard uniform, standing at the end of their bed for a few short moments before disappearing into the walls. Others say that Prior slams the cabinet doors in the kitchen at night. Paranormal investigation teams, though, say that Prior isn't the only spirit at Big Bay—they attribute the hauntings to at least five ghosts.

Another mysterious death haunts the lighthouses and grounds of Grand Island, just north of Munising in the chilly Lake Superior waters. The Grand Island East Channel Light is one of the most recognizable landmarks along the Upper Peninsula's Shipwreck Coast; the timber and brick structure began service in 1868 and ran for only forty years before becoming decommissioned. The structure has remained abandoned there since, only accessible by kayak or boat. Because of its haunting appearance of raw timber and slight decay, most passersby expect the East Channel Light to be home to a bevy of ghosts, but aside from a rare feeling of being watched or a glimmer of a shadow outside the building, this light is just a languishing reminder of the glory days in the Upper Peninsula's shipping era. The real ghosts haunt the Grand Island North Light, where an unsolved murder continues to plague the grounds.

The first lighthouse built on the North Light's spot atop a rocky cliff was a forty-foot-tall wooden tower, beginning its service in 1855. That lighthouse was replaced in 1867 by a brick tower and attached keeper's house. The North Light remains in operation today; it was automated in 1961. Now, though, the building is on private land and not open to the public.

In 1908, then head keeper George Genry and assistant keeper Edward Morrison went missing. The two left Munising to start the season at the light in late May, along with a boat packed full of groceries and supplies. Genry told his wife, who was staying behind in town, that he'd write to her in a week's time.

Grand Island's East Channel Light is one of the most recognizable landmarks in the Upper Peninsula.

A week passed, and Mrs. Genry hadn't heard from her husband. She decided to give it more time, just in case something had come up. After another week, though, she began to get worried. No one had heard from either Genry or Morrison. For Genry, this was unusual—he had been working the light for more than a decade and never let communication lapse between the couple. And reports were coming in that the North Light hadn't been operating in about a week. Mrs. Genry went to the sheriff, who put together a search party and went out to Grand Island. The search party had no luck finding the keeper and his assistant and reported the two men missing.

On June 12, 1908, the severity of the situation became clear. A small sailboat appeared off Au Sable Point, about thirty-five miles east of Munising and Grand Island. Morrison's body was found in the boat. The corpse was mangled; his head had been bashed beyond recognition, and his shoulders were equally crushed, as if beaten by some sort of club. Only Morrison's distinctive thirteen-star tattoo allowed investigators to identify the body. The official cause of death claimed by a coroner's jury was exposure to the harsh Lake Superior environment in his little boat. His date of death was placed at

June 7. After an investigation by a second coroner's jury, the cause of death shifted to include possible murder. Genry was still missing.

After the discovery of Morrison's body, another group of men sailed out to Grand Island to investigate the lighthouse. According to reports, Genry had been seen in Munising the day before Morrison's death, shopping for supplies and heading back out to the North Light. When investigators arrived at the lighthouse, they found those supplies still piled on the dock. Genry's coat was hanging nearby in the boathouse, and Morrison's vest was slung over the back of a chair. Everything appeared normal—Morrison had even made log entries in the logbook for June 5 and started one for June 6. The only thing suspicious was a missing boat (presumably the one Morrison's body was found in) and the still-missing head keeper.

Rumors sprang to life about what happened to the two men. The first was the most unlikely—that the men had gone out fishing, Genry fell in and drowned and Morrison floated about in the boat, not knowing what to do, until he became the victim of a Lake Superior storm. The kink in this story, though, is that Morrison was an accomplished sailor and had previously owned and operated his own sailboat.

The second, more sinister theory says that Genry murdered Morrison and then ran away to hide in Canada. Apparently, Genry wasn't the easiest head keeper to work with, and he and Morrison didn't exactly get along. A few days after his body was found, Morrison's wife received a letter he sent saying Genry was "quarrelsome" and opposing him might result in some sort of accident. Morrison was very explicit, telling his wife, "Do not be surprised if you hear of my body being found dead along the shore of Lake Superior." Did Morrison predict his own death? This murderous story says he did: the two began to argue as they were unloading supplies onto the dock. Furious, Genry bashed in Morrison's skull and then threw the man into a small sailboat and pushed him out to the lake. Genry planned to wait a few days until the body was sure to be claimed by Lake Superior and then say that Morrison deserted him. If the body were to wash up, though, Genry would say Morrison went out for a sail and never returned, so it must have been some horrible accident. Reports surfaced of Genry in Munising, drinking heavily, for the week after Morrison's body was found. Perhaps his wife hid him at home (and he escaped a few times to settle his soul with alcohol) before she saw his safe passage to Canada, where he could remain hidden from the law.

The third and most likely theory is that both men were murdered and pushed into the lake in their own boats. While Genry was in Munising on

June 6, he collected the paycheck for both himself and Morrison. Upon his arrival back to the dock on Grand Island, the two were robbed and murdered and their bodies set to sail in separate vessels. According to Genry's children, though, the murders had a different reason. The owner of the island at the time had a game preserve, and the animals would often wander onto the lighthouse property. Ever resourceful, Genry would shoot the animals and cook them for dinner. Well, the island's owner didn't appreciate that much and hired someone to kill Genry and Morrison and dispose of their bodies.

The double-murder theory seemed to be proven early in July that year when a body washed up by the Grand Island East Channel Light. Although the East Channel keeper claimed that it was Genry's body (the two were good friends), no positive identification was ever recorded. Further, no witnesses would corroborate the story of finding the body. To this day, it still hasn't been proven that it was Genry's body, and the murder (or murders) remains unsolved.

Of course, Genry is said to still haunt the lighthouse and the island. Mechanical things tend to break down on the north side of Grand Island—cars stall, appliances stop working and even lawnmowers and motorcycles just seem to give up. The islanders always blame it on Genry and his foul temper, who's either taking out his remaining anger from being killed or still crabbing about whatever he and Morrison got into a fight about.

Odd occurrences happened at the lighthouse even before the keeper's death. In 1872, eyewitnesses reported a black cloud hanging over the North Light on an otherwise pleasant day. Suddenly, a loud explosion rushed from the cloud, and it disappeared. Was it ghosts? Or maybe a UFO? Perhaps the lighthouse has been cursed ever since, and that could explain the deaths and disappearances.

The hauntings on Grand Island extend beyond the fate of the poor unfortunate light keeper. Reports abound of ghostly voices on the island, shadows running through peripheral vision and feelings of being watched. Investigators have picked up people talking on voice recorders while on the island—one team even caught the name "Abraham Williams" spoken from an unknown source. Williams was one of the first settlers on the island; he and his family arrived in 1840 and built a successful fur trading post. They owned most of the island until 1900, when he sold it to the Cleveland-Cliffs Iron Company.

If you listen carefully, those haunting voices may even tell you the location of one of Grand Island's greatest legends: the lost treasure sunk nearby.

The story goes that the steam ship *Superior* set sail from Sault Ste. Marie on October 29, 1856, carrying 216 barrels of whiskey and $30,000 worth of gold coins. The gold was meant to be salary money for the men working in the copper mines on the Keweenaw Peninsula.

The *Superior* would never make it to the Keweenaw though. That same night, at about 11:00 p.m., the steamer hit a severe storm off the coast of Grand Island. Icy waves destroyed the stack and cabins on the deck and took the rudder only half an hour later. The ship held on through the storm as it continued to the next morning, but the steamer's fate was sealed. A cry rang up among the crewmen, notifying everyone to rocks ahead. There was no way to avoid hitting them, so in his wisdom, the captain dropped anchor, hoping that would buy enough time for the crew and passengers to get ashore. But another massive wave tore apart the anchor chain, and the *Superior* was thrown ruthlessly onto the rocks along Grand Island's shore.

Only eleven of the forty-six aboard the vessel survived. By the time they were found, they'd been wandering around Grand Island for two days. None of the survivors had any idea anymore where the ship smashed onto the rocks, but they did recall the treasure now buried at sea: fifteen canvas bags full of gold coins, all contained in a safe now resting somewhere at the bottom of the lake.

THE TORTURED ORPHANAGE

Looking back, it seems like Holy Family Orphanage in Marquette didn't have the best of reputations from the start. Frederick Eis, a bishop with the Marquette Catholic Diocese, petitioned for the building's construction in the early 1900s, when the two other orphanages in the Upper Peninsula had reached capacity. The cost to build it—reaching up toward $120,000—was astronomical for typical expenses when it was erected in 1915. But it soon saw a return on that investment, becoming the region's biggest orphanage and housing up to two hundred children at once.

That's where the bad reputation comes in. Originally, Holy Family was meant just to serve white children who either lost their parents or were abandoned by them. That sounds bad enough on its own, but the first residents actually came as overflow from the orphanage in Assinins, which had a sordid past all its own. Eight nuns arrived in Marquette with control of

Before the Holy Family Orphanage became apartments, it languished in disrepair.

The old orphanage at Assinins before residents were moved to Marquette. *Michigan Technological University Archives and Copper Country Historical Collections.*

sixty Native American children, all of whom had been ripped from the arms of their parents in Assinins as babies in the continuing effort to assimilate native culture into white mainstream society. Locals today still tell stories of how their parents were stolen from their native families, placed in the orphanage and then adopted out to white families, never learning of their original heritage or customs until late adulthood.

And then came the allegations of abuse. When the orphanage was fully up and running, stories would leak out of children suffering at the hands of the nuns. It was a tough life, sure, with days filled by church, class and chores. But underneath the workaday existence was something much more sinister. Former children of the orphanage, once grown and moved out, often refused to speak of their time there, save to say that the nuns were cruel and inflicted unsettling punishments on the children. They heard of other children in the orphanage being beaten to death or left out in the cold Michigan winters.

One story that has been passed around but has only been somewhat proven is of a small girl who went out to play during a snowstorm. The weather quickly took a turn for the worse, and the girl became lost. One of the nuns had to rescue her, but by the time she got to her, the girl had developed pneumonia. She died a few days later. The nuns were still angry about her excursion out during winter and decided to make an example of her. They left the body on display in the lobby. Every child was forced to view the girl to be reminded about what could happen to them were they to disobey and go out in bad weather. Former residents confirmed that the death did indeed take place. The nuns held a funeral for the girl in the basement. None, however, would say whether the body was actually put on display.

Other reports tell of a young boy who suffered a mysterious fate. The general consensus is that he either drowned or was beaten to death, and the nuns tried to cover it up. They reported his death as accidental and stored his body in the basement.

Holy Family's checkered past means it's a magnet for ghost hunters and fans of the paranormal. Students from the nearby college would often head out there at night to try to experience something...and they usually did. One woman mentioned sneaking in with friends only to see an empty baby carriage mysteriously roll across the floor with no explanation. Others hear the sounds of children crying from the lobby where the little girl was left for everyone to see. And in the basement, where the boy's body was hidden, many have reported a glowing green orb encompassing a medical-style table. Locals frequently see lights flitting around inside the building after dark with no terrestrial explanation. In response to one paranormal team's research findings, a local resident claims to have gone with a medium. They were overcome with a freezing blast of air and a deathly smell that made the medium vomit.

The final orphans left the building in 1967, a group of Cuban refugee children fleeing from Fidel Castro's regime. In the 1980s, the building was completely abandoned, soon falling victim to a bankrupt owner who lived out of state and didn't want to sell. But as of late 2017, the orphanage has been purchased and remodeled and is now Grandview Apartments, a modernized building with fifty-six apartments and views of Lake Superior from the top floor. No word yet, though, on if the ghosts of the orphanage are enjoying the new digs too.

PART III

EASTERN UPPER PENINSULA SPIRITS

SPECTRAL SHIPWRECKS

At the eastern end of Lake Superior's southern shore, the Whitefish Point Light Station and Shipwreck Museum mark one end of the lake's "Shipwreck Coast." This roughly eighty-mile stretch of shoreline is also called the "Graveyard of the Great Lakes," and with good reason—about 550 shipwrecks dot the bottom of Lake Superior, and more than 200 of them happened off the coast of Whitefish Point. It's partially due to location. Here, the shipping lanes combine into a narrow pass-through as boats head from Sault Ste. Marie, through Whitefish Bay and out into the great lake. The deadly moniker is also thanks to weather in the area. Lake Superior is known for fierce gales, poor visibility and relentless waves. On many occasions, thick fog has caused ships to collide and ultimately sink.

A lighthouse first appeared at Whitefish Point in 1849, putting it in stiff competition with the Copper Harbor light for being the oldest in the Upper Peninsula. The original complex had only a stone tower and house for the lighthouse keeper and his family. But because the light was so isolated and on such a strenuous length of coastline, keeping a full-time tender at the station proved difficult. The first eight keepers all resigned. In 1861, a second light went up at the spot, connected to the light keeper's dwelling by a covered walkway on the second floor. More employees came to the light station in 1894, and the keeper's house expanded into a duplex, plus another home was built for a second assistant keeper.

A view of the Whitefish Point light station from the shoreline. *Author's collection.*

The Coast Guard arrived at Whitefish Point in 1923, establishing a lifesaving station due to all the deaths happening just off the coast. It was one of the most dangerous stations to work at, with frequent rescues so difficult that even the lighthouse keepers had to assist. Waves would carry in bodies of dead sailors, and in the winter, the corpses were chipped out of ice and pushed to the shore. Some of the most famous wrecks lie in the waters off Whitefish Point—including that of the *Edmund Fitzgerald*, which wrecked in 1975 and was immortalized in a Gordon Lightfoot song. The crew of the *Edmund Fitzgerald* was too late to be saved by the team at Whitefish Point. By that time, the light had been automated. The Coast Guard closed the station in 1951, and by 1970, all personnel had left.

Today, the Whitefish Point complex hosts the second of the lighthouses built, a museum inside the keeper's house, a bed-and-breakfast in the crew quarters building and a veritable graveyard of shipwreck paraphernalia in the Shipwreck Museum. The bell of the *Edmund Fitzgerald* itself is held in the museum, along with artifacts from the wrecked *Independence, Niagara, Comet, Drake* and more.

With all that death, it only makes sense that some spirits would hang on to the spot in the afterlife. Depending on who you ask at the facility,

Looking down on the Whitefish Point crew quarters from atop the lighthouse tower. *Author's collection.*

you may hear scoffing at haunting reports, but the stories are numerous and well documented. The Upper Peninsula Paranormal Research Society has done a number of investigations in the museum and on the lighthouse grounds, where it has heard and recorded mysterious voices in conversation and seen odd readings on equipment with no explanation. Ghostly footsteps and other unexplained sounds ring out through the entire property on a regular basis. Shadows move inside the lighthouse and past windows. Some investigators have reported a ghostly presence brushing past them in the middle of the night. In the light keeper's house, the investigation crew felt a huge pressure to leave the building, and it only got worse throughout the night. One investigation team, in town from Detroit, claims to have captured a full-body apparition on camera—twice. Near the *Edmund Fitzgerald*'s bell, the Northern Michigan University Paranormal Research Team decided to read off the names of those who perished in the wreck, and as the team spoke the name of the second cook, strange things began to happen.

"Our EMS detector, which detects electromagnetic fields and fluctuations, started spiking really severely," Lillian Konwinski, the team's chairwoman, told MLive. "That's when things started getting really interesting. Some people reported having their hair tugged, their faces being touched and arms being grabbed, but in an affectionate way."

One psychic who came to visit reported that at least fifty ghosts are haunting the Whitefish Point Light Station. A young Native American girl has been seen frequenting the museum, the gift shop and the fog house. Another young woman wanders with her across the complex grounds. A female adult from the 1890s has been seen standing outside the lighthouse lamp room staring off into the lake, and a child waves from the tower window. Employees at the complex report mysteriously flushing toilets and spectral visitors walking around the lighthouse and museum. And in the crew quarters, overnight guests report doors mysteriously popping open at exactly 6:00 a.m., someone sweetly stroking their face or back and apparitions of men in Coast Guard uniforms walking through the building. The ghostly occurrences extend to the shoreline as well; visitors and employees often report seeing translucent sailors standing helpless on the shore as a shimmery image of a ship, perhaps the *Edmund Fitzgerald*, floats past before disappearing into the mist.

"The idea of ghost ships on the Great Lakes is an old one, and it's not unique to the Lakes," Stonehouse said. "They're seen theoretically all over the world, but on the Lakes, it was common back in the 1880s up until maybe 1930 that if there was a storm on the Lakes and a ship was lost, especially with all hands, that other sailors would claim when the waves were

The *Edmund Fitzgerald* as it looked before its untimely sinking in Lake Superior's gales of November.

really getting up there and the fog was bad and the storm was blowing that they would see, at least for some seconds, the image of that same ship trying to complete its journey. And that was the complaint or the statements that were made about *Fitzgerald*."

Several other ships appear to haunt the coastline just off Whitefish Point. Take the *Lambton*, for example. The small lighthouse tender boat left Sault Ste. Marie in April 1922, heading into the icy waters of Whitefish Bay. It was carrying both lighthouse keepers and supplies, intending to deposit them along the Lake Superior shore. But the ice became too much. The *Lambton* was traveling with two other ships, the *Glenlivet* and the *Glenfinnan*. The *Glenfinnan* got stuck in the ice floating in the bay, and the *Lambton* helped to set it free. But as the ship came loose, the *Lambton* and the *Glenfinnan* collided, breaking the *Lambton*'s steering mechanism. The three ships stayed close to one another throughout the night to ensure that nothing bad happened. The next morning, though, a storm hit. The two *Glens* sought shelter in Whitefish Bay, but the *Lambton* turned north, looking for shelter there. It would be the worst decision that captain made. The storm ended that evening, and when the wreckage appeared, only the small pilothouse of the *Lambton* remained intact. Twenty-two passengers and crew were lost to the treacherous Lake Superior waters during that storm.

None of the bodies from the *Lambton* was ever recovered, but that didn't stop them from reappearing in Whitefish Bay in the following years. The spring after the storm, a lighthouse keeper and his wife both reported the ship appearing out of the fog and disappearing again. A fisheries employee saw it again later that year; he was out on a boat in the bay when the *Lambton* again emerged from the fog and then faded into nothingness.

The *Western Reserve* suffered a similar fate. In August 1892, the boat hit a storm near Deer Park, about thirty miles west of Whitefish Point. The ship was on the way to Two Harbors in Minnesota. Captain Albert Meyer decided to try and wait out the storm in the shelter behind Whitefish Point but eventually decided that the ship was strong enough and the storm weak enough that they could continue on their way and safely reach their destination.

By 9:00 p.m., Meyer was proven horribly wrong. A huge wind and horrible crash tore up from the surface of Lake Superior, splitting the *Western Reserve* in two pieces. The crew was able to get both lifeboats down and fill them with both passengers and sailors as the ship sank. It took less than ten minutes after the split for the *Western Reserve* to sink, and in the process, one of the lifeboats capsized. The second lifeboat came to the rescue but only managed to save two lives: the captain's son and the ship's steward. The lifeboat carried the only nineteen people who survived the shipwreck.

The fate of that second lifeboat, though, was just as dismal as the first. It turned toward Whitefish Point, hoping to make the sixty-mile row to safety on the shore. All went well until the boat reached about one mile offshore the next morning. The wind picked up and sent a considerable wave to the boat, capsizing it and drowning everyone within, save for one passenger: the *Western Reserve*'s wheelman, Harry Stewart. Stewart swam the mile to shore and then walked ten miles to the nearest lifesaving station at Deer Park, where bodies had already begun to wash ashore.

Captain Benjamin Truedell, the head of the Deer Park station, may have already known that Stewart was coming to report the tragedy. For a few nights before the *Western Reserve* sank, Truedell suffered from incredibly vivid nightmares. He dreamed that he was watching the *Reserve* sink and taking all the passengers and crew to the bottom of Lake Superior. He even saw bodies washing up along the shore, including that of Peter Minch, the wealthy financier who owned the *Reserve*'s fleet. Truedell knew that his nightmare had come true when he found Minch's body on the beach and recognized him from the dream.

But the *Western Reserve* still sails. People walking along the shore or visiting the lifesaving stations report seeing the boat emerge from a newly erupted wall of fog and waves. The ship appears when the weather is calm as well, carrying ghostly voices and laughter from the former passengers across the wind to the beach.

The most famous of the Great Lakes ghost ships, though, is the *Griffon*. It's more than three hundred years old and was the first European ship to sail through the Lakes. And it's been lost to history. The *Griffon* wrecked, and the remains were never found—since then, it's become the white whale of Great Lakes shipwreck hunters, "discovered" countless times only to have the wreck turn out to be something else.

"Everybody's got this...insanity [about finding it]," Stonehouse said. "It's fun because we keep finding it, everybody gets excited about it, and then of course it all just kind of fades back away into history. So maybe the ghost of the *Griffon* is really all these findings of people across the bottom of the lake, none of which, of course, turn out to be the *Griffon*."

Shipwreck hunters tend to find something they think is the *Griffon* every three or four years, but seasoned sailors know that the ship still runs on a ghostly route across the Lakes. Back when car ferries routinely plied the Great Lakes, they ran a similar route to what the *Griffon* would have sailed. The car ferry sailors often reported seeing the ship emerging through fog and then disappearing. Every time it was seen, bad weather followed. It became a sort of warning signal for rough seas.

One of the most haunted ships on the Great Lakes isn't a wreck, though. It's a permanently docked boat on the St. Mary's River in Sault Ste. Marie: the *Museum Ship Valley Camp*. The boat was built in 1917 and run as a freighter on the Lakes, carrying a crew of twenty-nine and loads of limestone, coal and iron ore. When the Soo Locks celebrated one hundred years of operation in 1955, the *Valley Camp* was the first ship through the locks, marking the beginning of the next century of service. By the time the ship was decommissioned in 1966 and subsequently relocated to its present spot along Water Street, it had covered nearly 3 million miles of water and carried more than 16 million tons of cargo.

Now the *Valley Camp* is the Great Lakes' largest maritime museum. Visitors are able to explore more than one hundred exhibits in the cargo hold, as well as the deck, the wheelhouse, the engine room and the crew quarters. Four aquariums on the ship showcase various fish species endemic to the Great Lakes, and one of the most compelling exhibits on the boat is the memorial to the *Edmund Fitzgerald* wreck. The *Valley Camp* has two of the mangled lifeboats salvaged from the ship's debris.

The *Valley Camp* is also a hotbed of paranormal activity. Investigation groups have been out to the ship numerous times, and nearly every time,

The *Valley Camp* was a freighter on the Great Lakes for fifty years and is now a museum.

Inside the *Valley Camp* sit two salvaged lifeboats from the *Edmund Fitzgerald* wreck. *Author's collection.*

Only half of this *Edmund Fitzgerald* lifeboat survived the sinking. *Author's collection.*

The mangled *Edmund Fitzgerald* lifeboats are a hotbed of paranormal activity. *Author's collection.*

they get some sort of evidence. Paul Sabourin, curator for the Sault Historic Sites, recounted in an interview for this book about the time Metro Paranormal Investigators came up from Detroit to do an investigation on the ship. The team recorded two ghostly voices. The first was caught near the *Fitzgerald* lifeboats, a man with a thick East Coast accent saying the name "George," which happened to be the name of one of the chief engineers who worked on the *Valley Camp* when it was in service. The second audio clip was recorded in the ship's dining room, with a clear view to the water. It was a calm day, and the river was completely flat. The voice on the recorder appeared to be noticing the exact same thing, saying just one word: "Flat." During another investigation of the boat, a different group caught an entire sentence. The team was working in the old coal room when it heard someone faintly coughing. One of the investigators quietly remarked that it sounded like coughing, and right away, a ghostly voice emerged from nowhere in particular to say, "I am coughing." And on yet another investigation, Sabourin said, a piece of coal came flying horizontally from out of nowhere, hitting one of the team members like someone threw it at him.

Outside the investigations, visitors report feeling like someone is following them, looking over their shoulder or speaking to them, especially as they get closer to the *Fitzgerald* lifeboats. People often see shadowy figures roaming the ship's deck outside in the middle of the night as well.

THE WATERFRONT

More than two thousand years ago, Native Americans came together on the banks of the St. Mary's River in what's now known as Sault Ste. Marie. They came for fish and fur and to trade with other area tribes. The original native settlers lived in homes built from wood poles and animal hides; they dubbed the area "Bahweting," which translates to the "Gathering Place." Missionaries and fur traders arrived from France in the 1600s—including Father Jacques Marquette, who established the first mission here in 1668, which was the first one in the entire state of Michigan.

The gatherings weren't always peaceful though. In 1674, the Ottawa and Huron tribes briefly joined forces to fight against the Sioux tribe. The three tribes met at Sault Ste. Marie, the Sioux under the impression that all would have a peaceful gathering. But one of the Ottawa and Huron group pulled out a knife, holding it in the face of one of the Sioux and calling him a coward. The Sioux man told the assailant he wasn't afraid and was then killed on the spot, the knife plunged into his heart.

Over the following century, Sault Ste. Marie was a constant battleground. The French and British, who both wanted rights to trade with the Native Americans, frequently fought for ownership of the land. But it was all for naught, as the 1820 Treaty of the Sault deeded the city to the United States. The army built Fort Brady shortly thereafter to deter infiltrations from the British waiting across the river in Canada. The fort was abandoned in the 1890s, though, and rebuilt on the spot that's now home to Lake Superior State University.

Thanks to aggressive rapids and a twenty-one-foot drop from Lake Superior to the lower Great Lakes, fur traders quickly realized the need for a set of locks on the St. Mary's River. It was getting tiresome unloading canoes and boats and hauling the cargo overland to meet the boat on the other side of the rapids. So, in 1797, the first lock opened, owned by the Northwest Fur Company. It was small, only thirty-eight feet long, and designed mostly for trade canoes. The lock was subsequently destroyed in the War of 1812, forcing overland cargo portage again.

Once Sault Ste. Marie came under American control and the state of Michigan was founded, campaigning began for a new lock. Two new 350-foot-long ones were built thanks to a Congressional land grant and opened in 1855, now named the State Lock. By the 1870s, the importance of the locks had become evident—a new, larger one was necessary, but the state didn't have the funds to build it. Michigan petitioned the federal government, and in 1881, a new lock was built and control was officially turned over to governmental power. The locks, now known as the Soo Locks and the busiest in the world with four working slots, have been managed by the U.S. Army Corps of Engineers ever since.

The waterfront along the river, close to the locks, has historically seen its share of troubled spirits and bodiless forms roaming across the land—whether it's the soul of a slain Indian, sailors lost in history to the fate of their boats or something more otherworldly. On multiple occasions, people on the ground in the Soo Locks Park have reported UFOs hovering over the locks. One pair of cops even followed the mystery object until it disappeared, only relating their story to a paranormal group, lest they be mocked by others on the force. The most famous UFO sighting, though, is the Kinross Incident.

In 1953, something unusual appeared over the Soo Locks. No one could identify what it was, just that it was hovering in restricted air space. The nearby Kinross Air Force Base was alerted to the intrusion and sent out

The *T. Hutchinson* passes through the Soo Locks on a cold winter day. *Library of Congress.*

a jet to intercept it. First Lieutenant Felix Moncla Jr. piloted the jet, while Second Lieutenant Robert Wilson manned the jet's radar. As the jet arrived at the locks, Wilson started having trouble tracking the object. Neither he nor Moncla could see it, so they relied on the radar operators in Sault Ste. Marie to guide them. Under the ground operator's direction, the jet closed in on the object—until the two blips on the radar merged into one single dot, which then floated up toward Canada and disappeared, taking the jet with it. The plane and its two-man crew were never seen or heard from again.

Did a UFO appear over the locks in 1953 and abduct two men and their jet? Perhaps only the unidentified objects seen by others in the area know.

In a more ghostly incident, paranormal tour leader Jim Couling was showing a group around the Soo Locks Park when he saw a man dressed in 1920s vintage walk up to the group and begin to listen. After a few moments, the man turned to a couple on the tour and asked, "Do you like gatherings?" The couple said yes, and the man asked again. He then walked in a slow circle around the couple and asked a third time before vanishing into thin air. On other tours, Couling and guests have heard disembodied laughter from spectral children and smelled cigar smoke wafting past when no one was smoking.

Two properties close to the waterfront also report strange occurrences. The Ramada Ojibway Plaza Hotel is said to be haunted by Beatrice, a woman who was either a housekeeper or the former owner's wife. Apparently, Beatrice likes to clean up—guests staying in the rooms that were once part of her suite tend to find their suitcases unpacked, clothes put away and the room made up fresh. The other spot, the former Windsor Park Hotel (which is now student residences), has a trick elevator. Whatever spirit lives on the fifth floor goes up and down quite a bit, a ghostly hand pushing the button to take them home. Former guests also reported unexplained footsteps, cold drafts and malfunctioning electrical items.

Still along the waterfront but about seventy-five miles by land to the west of Sault Ste. Marie, Crisp Point Lighthouse stands as another beacon of hope for mariners along the Shipwreck Coast. But this lighthouse isn't known for visions of ghostly ships—instead, the hauntings here are focused only inside the lighthouse and on the shore.

The facility at Crisp Point began just as a lifesaving station in 1876, housing lifeboats and Coast Guardsmen to help save drowning souls. In 1904, the lighthouse was built and officially lit. The entire property consisted of the lifesaving station and crew quarters, a duplex light keeper's house, a fog signal building, an oilhouse, two barns, a boathouse, a tramway, the lighthouse and a service room.

Crisp Point had a long and successful history of saving lives both on and off the water. In 1928, the then lighthouse keeper's son found a man wandering lost in a swamp and brought him back to Crisp Point. The man, Lou Williams, had spent three days lost. After he was rescued and brought back to health, Williams wrote a poem about the lighthouse and dedicated it to the keeper, Joseph Singleton:

CRISP POINT WATCH IS EVER

Roll Superior, cast thy strength; twisting, raging, turning.
But the Sailor knows no doubt or fear,
For through the night comes a glean of cheer—Crisp Point light is burning.
Rage Superior, spread thy fog, sleet, rain, and snowing.
But the Sailor sleeps in faith secure,
Though the stars are gone, the way is sure—Crisp Point horn is blowing.
Storm Superior, rage and roll. Spread thy vain endeavor.
Here no tale of death to tell—Crisp Point watch is ever.

The light was automated in the '60s and went completely dark in 1992. The tower and buildings were left to rot in the Lake Superior weather until the late '90s, when restoration work began under the Crisp Point Light Historical Society. In 2013, the light itself began operations again, acting as a seasonal beacon for private vessels. Now, volunteers who stay on the property overnight to greet visitors and handle repairs maintain the building.

Two ghostly stories haunt the Crisp Point Light. In one, three young men decided to stay overnight at the abandoned lighthouse on a hunting trip. This was before the lighthouse was saved and restored. They set up camp upstairs in the keeper's house. In the middle of the night, the three woke to the steady *thump* of someone walking up the stairs to the landing outside their open door. They hollered out that they were armed and had no problems shooting any intruder. When nothing responded but the sound of footsteps continuing to plod up the stairs, they let loose, raining bullets out the door with their rifles. Eventually, the footsteps stopped. Two of the boys fell asleep, but the third was too frightened and stayed up all night in the pitch dark just in case—and who knows what would have happened if he didn't, for when dawn broke, he heard footsteps on the landing again, only this time they were running back down the stairs and out the front door.

The other ghost haunting the Crisp Point Light is ominous in name and appearance: Three-Fingered Reilly. Reilly's story begins on the *John Owen* steamer. The boat, carrying a full load of wheat, got caught in a November gale and sank in 1919, taking all twenty-two crew members and passengers down for the ride. Four months later, a mailman running delivery along the coast in a dogsled found a body preserved in shore ice at Crisp Point. Crewmen came from the station to chop it out of the ice, accidentally severing two frozen fingers in the process. The man was later identified as William

Reilly, the assistant engineer for the *Owen*, and his body was kept frozen at the station as the team waited to hear about what to do with the corpse. But the weather warmed up a bit before they heard, thawing out the body but not enough of the surrounding landscape to get Reilly to a proper undertaker. He was buried in the cemetery at the light station. He never truly went to eternal rest though—starting shortly after his burial, visitors and workers at the station have reported footsteps right behind them, turning to see the ghost of Three-Fingered Reilly wandering the shore looking for his two lost digits.

In addition to the mysterious ghost on the steps and the phantom of Three-Fingered Reilly, Metro Paranormal Investigations picked up some strange recordings of activity at the Crisp Point Light. The group was out to do an investigation in August 2011, during a solar storm with gorgeous aurora borealis floating up above the light station. In its final case report, the group found nothing anomalous with photos, videos or personal experiences. But it did catch three ghostly whispers on the recorder: one saying "good afternoon," another saying "OK, be silent" and a third asking "Who are these people?"

HISTORIC BUILDINGS

Thanks to Sault Ste. Marie's distinction of being the oldest city in Michigan, it also has some of the state's oldest buildings—many of which are considered haunted. The John Johnston Historic Home is perhaps one of the greatest examples.

Johnston was a fur trader and one of the first full-time white settlers in the Soo. He arrived in 1793 with his wife, Oshahguscodaywayquay, who was the daughter of a local Ojibwa chief. The family built a stately log home overlooking the lower rapids of the St. Mary's River. The couple had eight children, and although Johnston took frequent trips for his fur trading business, the family lived a happy life on the banks of the river, surrounded by books, comforts from Johnston's native home of Ireland and the company of many visitors who came through the region. The Johnston home was known for hospitality and friendly welcomes to anyone who may pass by.

During the War of 1812, Johnston joined forces with the British (he was a loyal subject) and helped capture Mackinac Island. Two years later, he helped the British defend the island and keep it out of the hands of the Americans. But he returned to Sault Ste. Marie in 1814 to find disaster.

John Johnston was one of the first full-time white settlers in Sault Ste. Marie. This is his historic home. *Andrew Jameson.*

His home and business were in ruins, burned to the ground by a group of American forces that sailed up the river and ransacked his property.

The family quickly rebuilt the house, albeit smaller than the previous one, and in 1823, an extension was added for Jane, the oldest daughter, and her new husband, Henry Rowe Schoolcraft, the local Indian agent. Today, only the extension remains. The home is part of the Soo's Historic Water Street Homes Collection; visitors can learn about the fur trade, early life in the region and the Johnston family.

While you might expect Johnston himself, or even one of the couple's children, to be haunting the Historic Johnston Home, the ghost here takes on a more interesting form: Johnston's granddaughter Anna Maria, known to friends and family as Miss Molly. Miss Molly never lived at the Johnston home in Sault Ste. Marie. Instead, she spent her childhood homesteading Neebish Island with her parents and brother, about twenty-five miles south of the Soo. She founded a vacation resort there called O-Non-E-Gwud, which translated to the "Happy Place" in her grandmother's native Ojibwa.

In 1899, Miss Molly sold O-Non-E-Gwud to a professor from the Chicago area. She stayed on the island in her own cabin until her death in 1928, at which point her spirit promptly relocated to the Johnston home in Sault Ste. Marie.

She's been there ever since, watching over visitors to the ancestral home. She can be seen in fleeting glimpses passing by a doorway or felt standing behind you as you look at the family's belongings. She's even been known to have brief conversations with paranormal investigators visiting the house and is reportedly also the cause of unusual electromagnetic frequencies, infrared readings and some blurry apparitions caught on camera.

Sadly, Miss Molly likely never made it to the Antlers Restaurant in Sault Ste. Marie before she spectrally moved back into her family's home. If she did afterward, she may have made some ephemeral friends of her own that continue to haunt the popular family eatery.

The Antlers was built while Miss Molly was still alive in 1915, gracing the waterfront less than a mile from her grandparents' Water Street home. Back then, it was called the Bucket of Blood Saloon, a local watering hole for trappers, sailors and lumberjacks. When Prohibition hit in 1920, the owners changed the Bucket of Blood to a bucket of something much sweeter: ice cream. For a while, it took on the name North Star Ice Cream Parlor, although locals referred to it as the Bucket of Blood Saloon and Ice Cream Parlor.

In all honesty, the establishment was terrible at selling ice cream. Conservative estimates say that it only sold about one gallon of ice cream per month. Strange, then, that the business was still raking in about $900 in profits per month. Anybody would be suspicious—and the cops definitely were. The Bucket of Blood was eventually exposed for being a speakeasy and a brothel.

After Prohibition ended, the saloon went back to its former glory, sans the ice cream. It ran until 1948, when, ironically, two cops bought the place. Detroit natives Harold and Walter Kinney renamed the restaurant the Antlers and began to fill it with what it's now famous for: hundreds of taxidermied animals. They line the walls and the ceiling, grace the entrance of the restaurant and are even part of the décor—think a lampshade held up by a bodiless cow's leg.

Local legend says that the more than three hundred stuffed creatures inside were mostly obtained through the impressive bartering skills the Kinneys had. In the early days, trappers brought in animals and antlers in exchange for drinks, and a lumberjack looking for some booze therapy once even stopped by to leave a giant log as payment (this one, apparently, did not pan out). The most famous of the patrons was named Tiny, and he frequently brought in anything and everything just to get some alcohol—his contributions included a moose head, a gun and his car.

The restaurant today is owned by the Szabo family, who've kept up with the theme by serving unusual meats that visitors can eat under the watchful eyes of hundreds of animal corpses. Kids get free fake antlers to wear, and guests are often greeted by loud bells and hand-crank sirens still intact from the Prohibition days.

More than just the eyes of the staff and the beady optics of hundreds of animals usually watch diners at the Antlers though. It's considered one of the most haunted places in the Soo. Employees often report that some of the stuffed decorations—which are kept meticulously clean—move around overnight. A lady of the night and a waitress stick around from the restaurant's more sordid years, opening doors at random and playing around with office equipment, which tends to power on and off on its own. Several paranormal groups have investigated the building; during one investigation, an invisible force pushed one of the team members on a staircase by the kitchen. It's also been reported (and aired on the TV show *My Ghost Story*) that two more ghosts take up residence at the Antlers: a maintenance man and his wife. Supposedly he killed her and then himself on the property.

PART IV

MACKINAC ISLAND SPOOKS

UNTIMELY DEATHS

Dating as far back as AD 900, Native Americans inhabited small Mackinac Island in Lake Huron. It was considered a sacred place, home to the Great Spirit. Anishinaabe tradition says the Great Hare, Michabou, created the land in the natives' ancestral Mackinac Straits home. The local Indians thought the island resembled a large reptile when viewed from a distance, so they named it Michilimackinac, which translates to "Great Turtle." Eventually, it evolved to be simply "Mackinac." Because of its cultural significance to the local tribes throughout the Straits, Mackinac Island became the place tribes would go to bury their tribal chiefs, as well as serving as a spot for sacrifices to the gods.

The first white man to ever see Mackinac Island (that historians know of) was French Canadian fur trader Jean Nicolet in 1634, on an expedition for the government of Canada. He only passed through, though, on his way to find the Northwest Passage. Then the island remained untouched by outsiders for almost forty years, until the French came. Starting in 1670, Mackinac became a hub of the French fur trade. It would remain that way for about a century. After the French and Indian War, the British took over the Straits of Mackinac, eventually building Fort Mackinac on bluffs above the shoreline in 1780. Three years later, the Americans took over the fort; it was given to them in a treaty after the Revolution. But then came the War of 1812 and the British attempts to win back Mackinac Island.

Having seen at least two verified battles from the War of 1812, it goes without saying that there would be unintended casualties. One of the worst incidents remembered on the island happened at the beginning of the war. Mackinac Island residents weren't exactly aware that a war was really even going on yet, but that didn't stop the British forces from swooping in and fighting to claim the island for themselves.

At British Landing, a spot on the northwest side of the island, the British took their chance. It was here that they snuck ashore to surprise American forces in July 1812, about one month after the official start of the war. They hiked down to Fort Mackinac, working with Native American allies, and forced the Americans to surrender. This was easily accomplished, as the Americans had no idea they were being attacked or that the war had even begun. They surrendered without a single shot fired.

But farther around the north side of the island, another attack was happening. Some of the English forces took that route, running into a group of Native Americans. The British attacked, brutally murdering seventy-five Indian men. Now the ghosts of the attacked Indians haunt that spot. Locals

Not far from this spot on Mackinac Island, British soldiers slaughtered seventy-five Native Americans. *Library of Congress.*

and visitors both claim to have seen them running through the woods at night, trying to escape the slaughter waiting for them at the shore.

By 1814, the Indians on the island were fighting alongside the British. On August 4 that year, an American force attempted a sneak attack to retake the land. They came ashore at British Landing and began to advance inland. The trek took them to the farm of Michael Dousman, a fur trader who had initially arrived on Mackinac before the War of 1812 broke out. He was captured by the British in July 1812. The British army released him, though, on the condition that he not provide any intelligence to American forces. His compliance made him a strong ally for the Canadians and the British.

Perhaps owing to that alliance, the Americans encountered a large combined force of British and Canadian soldiers on Dousman's farm. They fought a bloody battle. In an attempt to outflank the British forces, the Americans tried to circle the line, but they weren't expecting the Indian forces hiding in the woods. They burst out, attacked the American forces and officially won the battle for the British.

Now a plaque marks the spot of the battlefield where many of the soldiers were buried where they fell. Spirits mark the spot as well; many visitors to this location report seeing apparitions of early 1800s soldiers, hearing shouts coming from the woods and noticing the ghostly screams of soldiers who perished in the battle.

After the War of 1812 ended, the island stayed under American control thanks to the Treaty of Ghent. Fur trading came and went, replaced by the fishing industry in the mid-1800s. Tourism grew, and the island became a quiet paradise for those looking to get away from the bustle of the city. The fort remained active until 1895; at that time, the State of Michigan made the majority of Mackinac a state park (the state's first), and the soldiers left the island and its Victorian charm to the tourists.

One of the most well-known untimely deaths on Mackinac Island was that of Corporal Hugh Flynn. Moments before his death in 1828, he had been arguing with Private James Brown in the mess hall at Fort Mackinac. Brown, sour from the disagreement, pulled out a musket and murdered Flynn on the spot. As the consequence of his actions, Brown's death became the first and only public execution on the island.

"He was hanged for murder, but not after a very long court case," Adam Franti, an interpreter at the fort, related to the *Mackinac Island Town Crier*. "He claimed it was an accident to the day he died, and you can trace Michigan's abolition of the death penalty back to this incident.

Even though most people seemed to think Brown was guilty, the island was a tight-knit community, even back then, and a lot of them had moral objections to hanging someone they all knew."

Brown met his fate on temporary gallows set up on the fort's rifle range, part of what's now known as Rifle Range Trail. The trail extends between Fort Holmes at the highest point of the island and Fort Mackinac closer to the shore. An apparition of Brown is said to haunt the trail, either still seeking vengeance from the argument or working to convince us still that the murder was a complete accident. Hikers along the trail have seen a full-body ghost wearing an old-fashioned uniform and have also reported someone tripping them or stepping on the backs of their shoes. And that's just the friendly, teasing occasions. Others report a bit of a meaner ghost that pulls hair and pushes people to the ground—if you listen closely, they say you can hear bullets firing and even feel them rushing past your face.

SPOOKY HOTELS

To this day, Mackinac Island retains both its charm and its otherworldly qualities. It's been called the most haunted island in the Great Lakes, ghost-infested and completely overrun with spirits. In 1898, a ban on vehicles on the island went into action, and now the only way around is on bike, on foot, by sled in the snow or by horse-drawn carriage. That's all thanks to carriage men of the past; they campaigned for the ban because they wanted to make sure engine noises didn't scare the horses. The highway that circles the island, Michigan 185, is the only one in the country that doesn't have motor vehicle traffic and the only one in Michigan to have never seen a car accident. It's only eight miles of road around the perimeter of the island, an easy trip many travelers tackle in one day.

Fudge shops proliferate Mackinac; there appears to be one around every turn, with many lining just Main Street alone. Some of the shops have been in operation for more than a century; the first opened in 1887, and the fudge industry gradually replaced the soldiers who remained on the island until 1895. Tourists coming for a taste of it have been (sometimes not-so-affectionately) nicknamed "Fudgies"—people who come for the day to eat the fudge, superficially explore the island and then head back on the ferry to the mainland.

As the fudge industry took hold on the island, so, too, did the many hotels and inns that still populate the village. Each of them has a storied history, and often that history includes the makings of a modern ghost story.

The Grand Hotel first opened its doors to business on July 10, 1887. It was constructed thanks to a combination of railroad and boating companies, which meant it already had a built-in advertising system. The lodging instantly became a hit, but it also took a monstrous amount of funding to run. By the early 1900s, the hotel had fallen on hard times. It was slated for destruction twice, each time saved by a new investor until it took off financially in the 1920s.

And then the Depression hit. Again, the hotel struggled to survive. In 1933, it went completely bankrupt, and the owners put it up for auction. Fate intervened in the form of Stewart Woodfill, an employee of the Grand since 1919. He purchased the entire building outright, keeping it afloat throughout the Depression and World War II, even during the bleakest times. At one point, Woodfill said that in peak summer season during these years, he had only eleven paying guests but four hundred working employees.

Main Street on Mackinac Island looks much the same today as it did in the early 1900s. *Library of Congress.*

Mackinac Island was and continues to be a bustling port of call for vacationers looking for a quiet getaway. *Library of Congress.*

Woodfill saw the hotel from tough times into rapid success. It became a hotspot for celebrities visiting Mackinac, who sometimes filmed movies with the Grand as the set. In 1957, under Woodfill's watch, Michigan selected the hotel as a State Historical Building. He sold the hotel in 1979 to Dan Musser, then the Grand's president, who had been an employee for nearly thirty years. Musser and his wife renovated and expanded the hotel, seeing it named a National Historic Landmark in 1989, and the Grand has stayed in the family since. It is now one of the top destinations on Mackinac Island—and reportedly one of the most haunted spots in Michigan.

The story goes that before construction of the hotel began, the original Post Cemetery was in the way of the proposed stables location and needed to be moved. But apparently, not all the bodies moved with the cemetery. As construction started, workers kept finding human skeleton after human skeleton, and not just in the old Post Cemetery spot. The entire area, it's said, was a known Indian burial ground. It got to the point where the construction

The Grand Hotel in 1900, one of the island's most haunted spots…if you can get anyone to talk about it. *Library of Congress.*

crews had unearthed so many bones that they simply put them back and built the hotel right over them.

Being built over several burial grounds goes a long way for instilling a spooky vibe in a hotel, and the Grand has the stories to match. Sure, there's the typical random footsteps, doors opening and closing on their own and feelings of being watched. But here, soldiers are said to wander through the hotel's halls with ghosts of Victorian-era adults and children, who also seem to haunt employee housing on the property. A man with a top hat appears to guests for one last concert in the piano bar, disappearing into a puff of cigar smoke and a lingering song. A Victorian woman likes to curl up next to employees when they go to bed at night.

And then there's the demon. Two maintenance men had a run-in with the evil entity of the Grand Hotel: a black shadowy mass with glowing red eyes. They were doing routine checks on the hotel's theater stage when one of them became overwhelmed with dread. He looked to the stage and saw the demon's eyes shining in the darkness, hovering in a cloud of black. The mass rushed at him, hitting him full on and throwing him to the floor. When the maintenance man woke up, it was two days later and he was in the hospital. He refused to ever return to the hotel.

The Grand, though, doesn't really like to talk about its ghostly friends (or enemies). Anyone who asks about them is usually told there's nothing paranormal, or the topic is expertly skirted. But if you get the right person, you'll hear tales galore—like the former chief bellhop, who once regaled friends with stories of full-body apparitions floating around the opulent space.

The Mission Point Resort is also considered to be one of the most active spots on Mackinac Island. Before any structure was built on the spot, Mission Point was used as a fishing camp location by local tribes. In 1782, a British captain built a small house on the spot, using it to entertain guests and other military acquaintances. After he was reassigned, the house was left abandoned and eventually collapsed.

Mission Point was reclaimed again in 1827, when an actual mission was built there, giving the spot its name. The mission ran for ten years. Afterward, the building was used as a hotel, the Mission House Hotel, for nearly one hundred years. The building was then sold in the 1950s and remodeled into a conference center and worldwide headquarters for the Moral Re-Armament, which alternately is called both a world peace organization and a cult. When the religious organization decided to leave in 1966, it gave the property to a new university, Mackinac College. Only one graduating class made it through the college, and since the early '70s, the property has been the luxury Mission Point Resort.

While Mackinac College had residence at the spot, a horrible tragedy occurred. One of the students, nicknamed Harvey at the request of his parents, who didn't want his actual name revealed, proposed to his girlfriend in the late 1960s. To his absolute heartbreak, she said no. Harvey grabbed a gun, went off into the woods behind campus and killed himself. That was in February; his body wasn't found until July, with two shotgun wounds to the head but no gun to be found. Some think that Harvey may have been murdered by the man his former lover was potentially cheating on him with, although the official reports say it was a suicide.

Harvey's heartbroken spirit never left the college, though, and remains to haunt Mission Point Resort. He's kind of a flirt too—he likes to hide in the theater and pinch or poke female visitors. Investigators have collected audio from the resort with a young man saying "shotgun" and "soundstage," where some believe the weapon was hidden if Harvey's death had been a

This 1843 sketch shows Mission Point long before it was developed with the arrival of white men.

murder. His ghost has been seen standing on the bluffs behind the resort, likely contemplating his last earthly moves.

Harvey also likes to play practical jokes on people at Mission Point. One woman reported that when she was alone in her room, the lights suddenly turned off and the bathroom door slammed closed. A former front desk supervisor fielded many calls from guests when he worked there in the late '80s, complaining of shadowy figures by their beds or in the halls. He even had an experience of his own; he was closing the resort down for the season and walking down a hall when, suddenly, all the doors behind him began slamming shut.

Other ghosts have appeared at Mission Point as well—soldiers and Native Americans are often seen walking around the grounds, an ethereal young girl known as Lucy calls out to her parents on a regular basis from different spots at the resort and an unknown woman in the theater both hums and sings aloud.

Unsolved murders seem to play a frequent role in haunted lodging on Mackinac Island. The Pine Cottage is another example. In 1942, a woman living at the house was brutally murdered; her case was never solved. Twenty years later, a man named Bob Hughey bought the cottage, and the murdered soul made herself known. It started small: ghostly footsteps, missing items, doors closing on their own, blankets being removed at night and so on. But then it took a turn for the macabre.

The Pine Cottage porch looks across to another haunted inn, Bogan Lane. *Pine Cottage.*

One day, Hughey walked into one of the rooms on the first floor and heard a ruckus coming from the closet. As he turned to look, the door sprung open, and a woman ran at him. Except it was only half a woman—everything was missing from the waist down. She ran straight through him, knocking him to the floor, and leaped out the window.

Things only intensified from there. Suddenly shadowy men were seen standing beside beds in the middle of the night. A little girl appeared, crying nonstop in nearly every room of the house, when before she'd only been glimpsed through the attic window. Current guests say the girl has blonde hair and was abandoned at the cottage by her parents. The scariest spirit is what some simply refer to as "the creature"—a thing that's rarely seen but appears as a hunched-over man with horns sprouting out his spine. The Hugheys could only take so much, and they bailed. The couple moved to St. Ignace in the '90s, but the ghosts of Pine Cottage still haunt the bed-and-breakfast today.

Half-chopped female ghosts don't seem to make an appearance at the Island House Hotel, though, which is the oldest hotel on Mackinac Island, built in 1852. Instead, there's a friendly old gentleman named Charlie who haunts these halls.

Inside Pine Cottage, one of Mackinac Island's many haunted establishments. *Pine Cottage.*

The Island House Hotel adds to Mackinac Island's collection of spooky spots, boasting several ghosts of its own. *Library of Congress.*

Charlie mostly chills on the fourth floor, a regular fixture in rooms 400 and 409. No one knows for sure who Charlie is, but locals have a theory that he once stayed in room 400 and died not long after leaving the hotel. Apparently, he loved it so much he wanted to return and plays pranks on the guests. In room 400, Charlie gets blamed for rearranging furniture, screwing with electronics and turning the shower on in the middle of the night. A housekeeper once reported that Charlie threw her cleaning bucket into the hallway; he must not have wanted her to interrupt his shower. In 409, Charlie likes to use the Jacuzzi tub. The door to the room will open and close on its own, and then the tub will randomly turn on.

The Michigan Area Paranormal Investigative Team, based out of Traverse City, once conducted a two-night investigation in the hotel and claims to have captured Charlie on camera. One of the photographs appears to show a man about five-foot-six, wearing a black overcoat and a top hat. The team also recorded whispering and something knocking in response to questions. Charlie also appeared to visit one of the investigators in room 407 in the form of a little white ball of light that appeared on a video camera. Once the investigator looked toward it, the light quickly flew out of the room.

ALL ABOUT WITCHES

Depending on who you ask, witch trials once reared their ugly head on Mackinac Island in the 1700s and 1800s. The story goes that a group of local women were working as prostitutes, luring married soldiers, fur traders and any other man who would have them into their homes for a bit of compensated fun. At once fearing for their reputation, the men declared the women witches who used their magical powers to seduce them.

The women were rounded up and taken away to the Drowning Pool, a lagoon between Mission Point and downtown on the Lake Huron side of the island. The site itself is very real and very dangerous. There's a twenty-foot drop at the bottom of the lagoon, with a lot of seaweed that has taken at least one life in the past—a man got tangled in it and drowned in the 1970s.

As for the witches, they were held to trial. Each one was tortured to try to get a confession. If no confession came, then came the water test. Similar to the Salem witch trials, the men conducting the investigation believed that witches would float, no matter what. Heavy stones were bound to the witches' legs, and they were thrown into the pool. If they floated, they were hanged as witches. If they sank, they were innocent—but dead anyway.

On the bright side, none of the women turned out to be witches, and thus their names were cleared of any wrongdoing—well, aside from the prostitution. But unfortunately for them (in addition to drowning) and the rest of Mackinac Island, their spirits are held deep within the Drowning Pool. People visiting the spot have seen dark shadows rising out of the water, with no noise or ripples to disturb the surface. Unexplained loud splashes, too big to be from fish, are a frequent occurrence. Some have even heard women whispering or screaming after midnight at the spot. The man who accidentally drowned appears to keep the accused witches company though. His apparition is often seen around the same time the women start to speak and splash around.

But according to Todd Clements, owner of the Haunts of Mackinac Tour Company, the happenings at the spot have nothing to do with witchcraft. "It was an urban legend started by several carriage drivers and has no historical accuracy," Clements said in an interview for this book. "The witch part is not correct. There are a couple reported drownings in the small pool of water and there is some strange activity, but nothing to do with a witch execution or curse. The legend is cool, but it never really happened." Unless, of course, he's been bewitched to say that.

Although it wasn't quite witches who haunted the spot on the southwestern side of Mackinac Island, Devil's Kitchen has a long and fabled history behind it. The cave formation looks like a Dutch oven, caused by eons of water smashing into it and hollowing out the spot. The weird thing, though, is that the inside of the cave appears to be covered in soot—like a wood-burning oven in someone's kitchen. Devil's Kitchen is one of the many rock formations on the island but also the youngest, formed around 350 million years ago.

Local Native American legend says the cave was actually home to a group of cannibal giants called the Red Geebis. There was a great battle between the Red Geebis and an Indian girl named Willow Wand. The legend goes like this: An old man named Aikie-wai-sie and his granddaughter, Willow Wand, were accidentally left behind on Mackinac Island one winter while the rest of the tribe left for the season. Willow Wand's beloved, Keweenaw, was expecting her on the mainland with the rest of the tribe. But since she was unable to make it, she left a signal for him: a white deerskin with red spots hanging from a cliff, so he would know to come find her.

The Devil's Kitchen caves are the home of legendary cannibal giants on Mackinac Island. *Library of Congress.*

Aikie-wai-sie and Willow Wand stayed on that cliff in hopes of rescue, which happened to be above Devil's Kitchen. Willow Wand knew the Red Geebis inhabited the cave, roasting and eating any human who dared venture too close. The two had to stay out of sight in order to survive, which unfortunately meant they could not go down to the lakeshore for water or to find food. They fell into a period of fasting, remaining up on the ledge struggling to survive without food or water while they listened to the Red Geebis murdering people below every night.

What Willow Wand didn't know was that she had magical powers: she could summon water by touching rock. But her powers would only appear after a great fast. After seven days stranded on the ledge, Willow Wand struck the rock in frustration, shouting out "Water!" As soon as she did, a spring of pure water burst forth from the rock. She and her grandfather were finally able to drink.

That evening, Aikie-wai-sie and Willow Wand were still stuck on the ledge waiting for rescue when the Red Geebis began their party of slaughtering below. Willow Wand peered over the edge of the cliff and spotted a familiar face: her beloved Keweenaw, being herded into the cave to be cooked and eaten. He had seen her signal and had come to save her but had been captured by the cannibals. In a rush to save his life, she began shouting and laughing, mocking the Red Geebis. The chief of the cannibals retaliated, coming up onto the ledge to steal Willow Wand down below and eat her as well. At that moment, Willow Wand slammed her fist down onto the rock, again shouting "Water!" and released a spray so strong it drowned out all the cooking fires in the cave below. She let loose a mist to disguise Keweenaw in his climb up to safety and then headed into Devil's Kitchen to throw all the Red Geebis out into the lake, drowning them and saving the island from the terrorizing cannibal giants for good.

Whether the legend is actually from natives on the island remains up for debate. The name "Devil's Kitchen" doesn't appear in the history books until the 1800s, and many believe that overzealous tour guides looking to give a good show fabricated both the story and the name. The soot on the inside is easily explained by tourists who headed to the cave in the 1920s to roast marshmallows and watch the water. But still today, people biking around the island or stopping in the caves report hearing the screams of unfortunate souls being cooked alive and the laughter of the cannibal giants as they wait for their meal.

FROM THE FORT TO THE DOCKS

All told, Mackinac Island has had more than one hundred reported ghost sightings, and that number continues to rise every year. Spirits inhabit every inch of the island, from the fort to the docks and everywhere in between. The ghosts even seep out into the Straits of Mackinac, like that of the spectral ship *W.H. Gilcher*.

The *W.H. Gilcher* was the sister ship of the ill-fated *Western Reserve*, built only a year later and sinking just two months after the *Reserve* went down. The ship and its crew of twenty-one were last seen alive on October 28, 1892, passing through the Straits of Mackinac on the way to Milwaukee. A storm was raging on Lake Michigan, and when morning came and the seas abated, the *Gilcher* was gone. All that remained of ship and sailors was a debris field floating near the entrance of Lake Michigan from the straits.

But like the *Western Reserve*, the *W.H. Gilcher* still sails. Reports come in to this day of the ship appearing in the straits among fog rolling off Mackinac Island. When the sea is calm and the sun is shining, Captain Lloyd Weeks again appears at the wheel, and a ghostly fog whistle blows toward the shore.

Back on land, historic areas of the island report their own hauntings. The Edward Biddle House, for example, is the oldest structure on the island, built back in about 1780. But Edward, a fur trader from Nova Scotia (although his family was originally Philadelphia royalty), wasn't the first owner of the home; before he purchased it, the house was owned by John Ogilvy (who likely built it), John Campbell and Robert Dickson. Biddle bought the house from Dickson in 1831, but he and his family likely lived in it as renters since 1822.

Biddle came to Mackinac Island in the early 1800s and decided to settle there after the War of 1812. He married a local woman, Agatha de LaVigne, who had mixed Ottawa Indian and French Canadian ancestry. They were both of relatively high stature on the island; Biddle dabbled in politics and ran an independent fur trading business, and Agatha was considered one of the local Indian chiefs. The couple routinely invited the sick and elderly of the Ottawa tribe into their home for hot meals, joining the couple's four biological children and many foster children. The youngest of the Biddles' children, Mary, died when she was only eight. In the winter, she was crossing the ice from Mackinac Island to St. Ignace. The ice wasn't completely frozen, though, and she fell through. She spent a week in the hospital and then died from pneumonia. Her grave is one of the oldest known on Mackinac Island and the oldest in St. Ann's Cemetery. In both 1831 and 1844, Edward was elected warden of the Borough of Mackinac, which was essentially like being the mayor. Agatha often managed the family fur business herself from inside the home.

During the time the Biddles lived in the house, Agatha saw her home island transform from being majority Native American to minority. She saw the native culture transformed thanks to white men and the appropriation of

This home was owned by Edward Biddle, a merchant from the East Coast who moved to Mackinac after 1812. *Library of Congress.*

Indian lands. She was present when the Treaty of Washington was signed in 1836, ceding millions of acres of native lands to the government in exchange for small reservations throughout Michigan.

"Agatha is watching all this," Eric Hemenway, archives and records director for the Little Traverse Bay Bands of Odawa Indians, told the *Lansing State Journal* in an interview about the Biddles. "Without a doubt, she was right in the thick of it as one of the chiefs of the Mackinac band."

After Edward and Agatha passed away, the house was deeded to their daughter Sarah. But under her ownership, it deteriorated and fell into disrepair. Mackinac State Historic Parks took it over in the 1940s and restored it to the cozy living space and museum it is today.

Now, visitors touring Fort Mackinac can also explore the Biddle House with a valid fort ticket. That ticket might also get them a chance to explore the paranormal, as the Biddle House is home to several mysterious occurrences on the island. Reports say that when the house is empty, people on the street hear voices and footsteps coming from inside. In other stories, a ghost is seen wandering around outside the house, although no one knows who it is. Perhaps it's one of the hundreds of ghosts haunting the island, or just little Mary, trying to find her way back home from the cemetery.

Mary may be buried at St. Ann's Cemetery (a spot she is said to haunt), but Fort Mackinac's Post Cemetery has a much spookier vibe. No one is exactly sure when the cemetery began, but the U.S. Department of Veterans Affairs notes that burials can officially be traced back to at least the mid-1820s. Locals, though, say the cemetery has burials of both British and American soldier casualties from the War of 1812. It's located about a half mile north of Fort Mackinac, across the street from St. Ann's Cemetery and just north of Skull Cave, which was a Native American burial site. A white picket fence surrounds the land, with an arched wooden entrance. There are 108 interments at the cemetery—though only 39 of those graves' inhabitants are identified. Burials stopped here in 1895, when the last of the soldiers left Fort Mackinac. But in honor of those occupying the hallowed grounds, the cemetery's flag continues to fly at half-mast, one of only four cemeteries in the country that hold that distinction.

Few civilians are buried in Post Cemetery, as is tradition with military graveyards. But of those who are there, many are children. One of the main hauntings reported at the cemetery is a woman, sitting forlornly in the back-left corner and weeping bitterly for the children she lost. Local legend says that woman is the mother of Josiah and Isabel Cowles, buried in Post Cemetery in 1884 and 1888, respectively. The two children both fell ill as

Visitors to Post Cemetery can hear ghostly sobbing coming from among the gravestones. *Library of Congress.*

toddlers, and medicine at the time could not cure them. Amid their mother's cries as she repeatedly watches them die and be buried can be heard the wailing of both small children as they suffer from their illnesses.

The road to Post Cemetery appears to be some sort of nexus for spiritual activity—how can it not be, connecting to three different cemeteries (the Lutheran cemetery is here as well) *and* an Indian burial ground? Locals try to steer clear of the area late in the evening, thanks to phantom horses among other things. Every night at about 3:00 a.m., the steady *clip-clop* of a horse-drawn hearse can be heard heading slowly up the road, yet another burial in tow.

BIBLIOGRAPHY

ABC10. "Ghost Haunts the Marquette Harbor Lighthouse." June 13, 2014. Abc10Up.com.

———. "Nahma Inn's Haunted Reputation Explored." July 11, 2017. Abc10Up. com.

Akamatsu, Rhetta. "Ghost to Coast Tours and Haunted Places." 2009. Lulu.com.

Aurora Daily Express. "Deluge of Death." September 30, 1893.

Beeler, Jennifer, Steve Millburg and Mamie Walling. "Top 15 Haunted Lighthouses." N.d. Coastalliving.com.

Beitler, Stu. "Calumet, MI Italian Hall Disaster Theater Panic, Dec 1913." N.d. Gendisasters.com.

Berger, Todd R., and Daniel E. Dempster. *Lighthouses of the Great Lakes: Your Guide to the Region's Historic Lighthouses.* N.p.: Voyageur Press, 2010.

Brand, Machabe. "British Aspect of the Battles of Mackinac Island, 1812 and 1814." Michigan Technological University, October 10, 2015.

Buchmann, Nicole. "Grandview Marquette Opens Doors." WLUC, Upper Michigan Source, November 10, 2017.

Carlisle, John. "Ghostbusters Chase the Unexplained in the U.P." *Detroit Free Press,* August 30, 2015.

———. "Mysterious Light Draws Thrill Seekers to a U.P. Forest." *Detroit Free Press,* May 16, 2017.

Carnacchio, CJ. "Ghost Tales, Haunted Houses Sought for OCTV Program." *Oxford Leader,* October 8, 2014.

City of Sault Ste. Marie. "Welcome to the Historic Water Street Home Kemp Industrial Museum." N.d. https://www.saultcity.com/historic-homes-1.

Courtner, Ellis W. "Michigan's Copper County." N.d. Michigan.gov.

Crain, Mary Beth. *Haunted Christmas: Yuletide Ghosts and Other Spooky Holiday Happenings.* Guilford, CT: Globe Pequot Press, 2010.

BIBLIOGRAPHY

Creager, Ellen. "Ghostly Guests: Some Michigan Hotels—and Owners—Haunted by Spirits." *Detroit Free Press*, October 21, 2016.

Elting, John Robert. *Amateurs, to Arms!: A Military History of the War of 1812.* Cambridge, MA: Da Capo Press, 1995.

Exploring the North. "A First Hand Report on the Haunting of the Eagle Harbor Lighthouse, at Eagle Harbor in the Upper Peninsula of Michigan (Keweenaw Peninsula), on Lake Superior." N.d. Exploringthenorth.com.

Fletcher, Ruth. "Could Bits Belong to Lambton?" November 1, 2011. Saultstar. com.

Fy, Andrew. "Paulding Light." *Atlas Obscura,* June 17, 2009.

Ghost Hunting with U.P.P.R.S. Video, Keweenaw, n.d.

Gmiter, Tanda. "1913 Italian Hall Disaster Was Michigan's Biggest Christmas Eve Tragedy." December 18, 2017. MLive.com.

———. "Tragic Anniversary: Girl, 7, Disappeared into Upper Peninsula Mine Shaft." July 21, 2017. MLive.com.

Godfrey, Linda S., Mark Sceurman and Mark Moran. *Weird Michigan: Your Travel Guide to Michigan's Local Legends and Best Kept Secrets.* N.p.: Sterling Publishing, 2006.

Goings, Aaron, and Gary Kaunonen. *Community in Conflict: A Working-Class History of the 1913–14 Michigan Cooper Strike and the Italian Hall Tragedy.* East Lansing: Michigan State University Press, 2013.

Goodrich, Marcia. "Just in Time for Halloween: Michigan Tech Students Solve the Mystery of the Paulding Light." *Michigan Tech News*, October 28, 2010.

Hambleton, Elizabeth, and Elizabeth Warren Stoutamire. *The John Johnston Family of Sault Ste. Marie.* Williamsburg, VA: John Johnston Family Association, 1992.

Havighurst, Walter. "Three Flags at Mackinac." *American Heritage* (August 1978).

Holmes, Christian. *Company Towns of Michigan's Upper Peninsula.* Charleston, SC: The History Press, 2015.

Hough, Lucy. "Residence Hall Rumors: Hatchet Man." *Northern Tradition*, December 6, 2012.

Hyde, Charles K. *The Northern Lights: Lighthouses of the Upper Great Lakes.* Detroit, MI: Wayne State University Press, 1995.

Jacobson, Ryan. *Ghostly Tales of Michigan.* N.p.: Adventure Publications, 2010.

Jean, Mark, and Terry L. Smith. *Haunted Inns of Amers—Go and Know: National Directory of Haunted Hotels and Bed and Breakfast Inns.* N.p.: Crane Hill Publications, 1999.

Johnson, Coralie Cederna. "Mysteries of the Michigamme." *Wildwood Press*, August 19, 2007.

Kandell, Jonathan. "The Wonderful Wildness of Michigan's Upper Peninsula." *Smithsonian Magazine* (May 2011).

Kendallville Standard. "Twenty-Eight Dead: Buried in a Mine Under the Michigamme River." October 6, 1893.

Keweenaw Report. "Ghost of Madame Modjeska: The 'Special Guest' of Calumet Theater's Gala Saturday." March 29, 2016.

Kleen, Michael. "Top 10 Most Haunted Theaters in the Midwest." *Mysterious Heartland*, May 12, 2014.

Langan-Peck, Jessica. "America's Top 10 Haunted Hotels." N.d. Frommers.com.

BIBLIOGRAPHY

Lavey, Kathleen. "Mackinac Island Restores Its Native American History." *Lansing State Journal*, March 7, 2017.

Lighthouse Friends. "Grand Island Lighthouse." N.d. Lighthousefriends.com.

Links to the Past—Wisconsin Genealogy and History Resources. "Great Lakes Maritime History of the Great Lakes." N.d. Linkstothepast.com.

Magnaghi, Russell M. *Prohibition in the Upper Peninsula: Booze & Bootleggers on the Border.* Charleston, SC: The History Press, 2017.

———. "Understanding Two Centuries of Census Data of Michigan's Upper Peninsula." Marquette: Northern Michigan University, Belle Fontaine Press, 2007.

Maine Ghost Hunters. "The Lost Souls of the Old City Orphanage." January 1, 2013. http://www.maineghosthunters.org/blogs/2013/01/01/the-lost-souls-of-the-old-city-orphanage.

Marquette Maritime Museum. "Marquette Maritime Museum Commemorates Lake's Legacy." N.d. Miningjournal.net.

Michigan Department of Transportation. "Mansfield Rd./Michigamme River." N.d. Michigan.gov.

Michigan State University. "Michigan's Copper Deposits and Mining." N.d. http://geo.msu.edu/extra/geogmich/copper.html.

Mines, Minerals and More. "Mansfield Mine, Crystal Falls, Menominee Iron Range, Iron Co., Michigan, USA." N.d. Mindat.org.

Mining Artifacts. "Michigan Copper Mines." N.d. Miningartifacts.org.

Misner, Marcy. "The Antlers: 100-Year-Old Landmark Restaurant." March 17, 2014. EUPNews.com.

Nahma Township Historical Society. "A Timeline of Historical Events in Nahma Township." December 2010. Nahmatownship.us.

Pattskyn, Helen. "Seul Choix Lighthouse One of the Scariest Places on Earth." November 29, 2016. Americashauntedroadtrip.com.

Peter White Public Library. "About the Peter White Public Library." N.d.

Pohlen, Jerome. *Oddball Michigan: A Guide to 450 Really Strange Places.* Chicago: Chicago Review Press, 2014.

Robinson, John. "Haunted Michigan: The Many Ghosts that Dwell in the Calumet Opera House." 99.1 WFMK, April 8, 2017.

Rudine, Ken. "The Keeper of Seul Choix Point." October 2, 2005. Texasescapes.com.

Schneider, Kim. "Eastern U.P.: Ghostly Presence Left at Lighthouse Crew Station B&B." June 16, 2018. MLive.com.

Seeing the Light—Lighthouses of the Western Great Lakes. "Keepers of the Eagle Harbor Light." N.d. Terrypepper.com.

———. "The Story of H. William Prior." December 17, 2003. Terrypepper.com.

Sellman, Mike. "Local Ghost Hunters Look Toward Helping More People." October 26, 2016. JCdailyunion.com.

Shiel, Lisa A. *Haunted Cooper Country: The History & Ghost Stories of Michigan's Keweenaw Peninsula.* N.p.: Jacobsville Books, 2015.

Singal, Jesse. "A University Threatened to Punish Students Who Discussed Their Suicidal Thoughts with Friends." Conde Nast, The Cut, September 22, 2016.

BIBLIOGRAPHY

Spokane Daily Chronicle. "Forty-Five Lost: A Cave-In at the Mansfield Mine Buries Alive Many Helpless Miners." September 29, 1893.

Spry, Adam. *Our War Paint Is Writers' Ink: Anishinaabe Literary Transnationalism.* Albany: State University of New York Press, 2018.

Stampfler, Dianna. "Meet the Keepers Who Remain within Michigan's Haunted Lighthouses." *Pure Michigan,* March 16, 2018.

The Standard Guide: Mackinac Island and Northern Lake Resorts. N.p.: University Microfilms International—Books on Demand, 1989.

Stonehouse, Frederick. "Do Ghost Walk at Whitefish Point? Paranormal Experts Investigate." *Lake Superior Magazine* (October 1, 2007).

———. *Haunted Lakes II: More Great Lakes Ghost Stories.* N.p.: Lake Superior Port Cities, 2000.

———. "Three-Fingered Reilly." *Lake Superior Magazine* (October 13, 2016).

Substreet. "The Abandoned Holy Family Orphanage, Marquette, MI." https:// substreet.org/holy-family-orphanage.

Tichelaar, Tyler R. *Haunted Marquette: Ghost Stories from the Queen City.* Marquette, MI: Marquette Fiction, 2017.

———. *My Marquette: Explore the Queen City of the North, Its History, People, and Places with Native Son.* Marquette, MI: Marquette Fiction, 2011.

Toler, April. "Campus Legends Range from Sweet to Sinister." Bloomington: Indiana University, 2014.

Travel the Upper Midwest. "Graveyard of the Great Lakes." February 27, 2018. Midwestweekends.com.

Usitalo, Kath. *100 Things to Do in the Upper Peninsula before You Die.* St. Louis, MO: Reedy Press, 2017.

Vachon, Paul. *Michigan's Upper Peninsula.* N.p.: Avalon Travel Pub, 2015.

———. "Unique Michigan Destinations on the Upper Peninsula." July 15, 2015. Moon.com.

Weingart, Marc. *Island of Adventure: Tales of Grand Island.* N.p.: Xlibris, 2002.

Wils, Karen. "House of Ludington Witnessed Esky History." *Daily Press,* August 21, 2015.

Wilson, Kay. "Fw: [GLSHIPS] Propeller St. Clair, Burning July 1876." E-mail reprinted in a mailing list, August 30, 1999.

Winsor, Justin. *Narrative and Critical History of America: French Explorations and Settlements in North America and Those of the Portuguese, Dutch and Swedes, 1500–1700.* N.p., 1886.

ABOUT THE AUTHOR

J ennifer Billock is an award-winning writer, bestselling author, editor and
owner of the boutique editorial firm Jennifer Billock Creative Services.
She has worked with businesses and publishers including Yahoo Travel,
National Geographic Traveler, Disney Books, *Porthole Cruiser*, Kraft Foods, *Midwest
Living*, Arcadia Publishing, the MSU Press and *Taste of Home* magazine. She
is currently dreaming of an around-the-world trip with her Boston terrier.
Check out her website at www.jenniferbillock.com and follow her on Twitter
@jenniferbillock.

Visit us at
www.historypress.com

Printed in the USA
CPSIA information can be obtained
at www.ICGtesting.com
LVHW080824011123
762556LV00006B/132